DEAR SIS:
Letters to a Queen

DEAR SIS:
Letters to a
Queen

DR. LATOSHA BURCH

SUFFOLK, VIRGINIA

Dear Sis: Letters to a Queen

Copyright © 2021 by Dr. Latosha Burch
All rights reserved.

All rights reserved. This book is protected by the copyright laws of the United States of America. This book may not be copied or reprinted for commercial gain or profit. The use of quotations or occasional page copying for personal or group study is permitted and encouraged. Permission will be granted upon request.

Final Step Publishing, LLC
PO Box 1441
Suffolk, VA 23439
www.finalsteppublisher.com

Soft cover ISBN: 978-1-7355280-9-0

For Worldwide Distribution. Printed in U.S.A.

Dedication

This book is dedicated to my mom, the late Sylvia W. Palmer, and the beautiful women who loved and encouraged me. I also dedicate it to those who sought to break me because you fueled my determination. Sisters uplift one another and stand as Queens. Whether your footprint in my life has been for a reason, season, or a lifetime, I am thankful for it all. May this book be a blessing to you and your loved ones.

Acknowledgments

Writing, in general, comes easy, but writing with a purpose and message comes with ebbs and flows of life experiences. It took me more than forty years to get to this point where I could share words of love and inspiration with women around the world. None of this would have been possible without my Lord and Savior, my loving parents (Del and Sylvia), grandparents (Matthew Sr. and Cora, Ulysses and Annie Mae), beautiful children (Jayla, Ramon, Tyler, Craig Jr., and Shanell), and my husband and teddy bear (Craig Sr.) They believed in me from the beginning and motivated me to be the best version of myself. I am also thankful for my family and friends near and far who have journeyed in life with me. I also thank my church family, St. Mark Missionary Baptist Church, and a special shout out to the Women of Praise, Diaconate, Bishop and Mrs. Evelyn Edmonds, and Pastors Dr. D.S. Riddick II and Dr. Jennell Riddick. You helped position me in ministry to stretch beyond what this southern country girl imagined. God used each of you to show me possibilities in life, and for this, I am forever grateful. I am stronger, wiser, victorious, #B.A.D. (blessed, anointed, and delivered), and #WHHF (whole, happy, healthy, and free).

I love you all and pray that God will bless you beyond measure.

Contents

Preface	1
Introduction	3
Letter 1: Hurt from the One You Love	5
Letter 2: Overlooked for a Job	9
Letter 3: Church Hurt	12
Letter 4: Sexual Assault & Abuse	15
Letter 5: Friendship	18
Letter 6: Decision-Making	20
Letter 7: It's Not Too Late	22
Letter 8: Self-Esteem	25
Letter 9: Love the Skin You're In	27
Letter 10: Accentuate the Positive	29
Letter 11: Death & Grief	31
Letter 12: Toot Your Horn	33
Letter 13: They Won't Support Me	35
Letter 14: Now You Know You Were Wrong!	37
Letter 15: No to Negative Energy	39
Letter 16: Health Care Treasures	42
Letter 17: What a Difference a Smile Makes	44
Letter 18: The Power of Laughter	46
Letter 19: I'm Not Superwoman	48
Letter 20: I am Happy for Her but Envious	51
Letter 21: Peeling Off Layers	53
Letter 22: Lonely in the Crowd	56
Letter 23: Eternal Security: Rooted in Christ	58
Letter 24: Don't Try Me; Try Jesus!	61

Letter 25: Build Your Faith Muscles 63
Letter 26: They Can't Stop My Shine 67
Letter 27: Don't Be Scared; Lean into It 70
Letter 28: Unexpected Love 72
Letter 29: Sister Circle 78
Letter 30: You Can't Stop My Praise 80
Letter 31: I Love you, But Sometimes You Pluck My Nerves! 83
Letter 32: Check Their Motives & Yours 87
Letter 33: Anxiety Sucks, But You Are a Conqueror 90
Letter 34: The Power of Words 92

EXERCISES

Self-Love Inventory

Celebrate A Queen Calendar

Crossword Puzzle: Building Faith Muscles
   Solution

Maze Exercise: It's All About Direction
   Solution

Fallen Phrases Exercise: The Power of Words Puzzle
   Solution

Bible Translations

References

About the Author

Preface

The Lord has given me many gifts and one is compassion for people. In my life's journey, I have always found myself encouraging, praying for, celebrating, and uplifting my sisters. Am I perfect? Absolutely not! However, I know how it feels to need a word of encouragement, a shoulder to lean on, or a listening ear from someone genuine. Through life lessons, I have come to know that one of my directives from the Lord is to help uplift women using the tools placed before me. I am a gifted writer, and it is one of the tools received to better communicate what God has laid upon my heart.

    I heard the voice of the Lord speak clearly telling me that I have stalled long enough, and it was time for me to write a book that would minister to other women. He spoke the title and topics, reminding me of my life experiences and those I have encountered. What he shared was further confirmed during a women's conference right before things shut down for the COVID-19 pandemic. After a beautiful conversation with one of my sisters in Christ and a friend that December, I committed to putting pen to paper that week.

    The saying "I am my sister's keeper" is not just a cliché; it holds meaning and has a broad spectrum of things we are to do towards one another. Queen is another term that once seemed purposed for royalty or those considered elites, but I have come to know that *we are all queens*. We are sisters linked by way of Jesus's blood, and because of this, it is necessary to spread love to one another.

    This book of letters was written to meet my queen sisters wherever they are in life and provide encouragement.

This is not your typical feel-good book, but it is designed to bring truth and inspire you to walk in greatness with all God has blessed you with. There are thirty-four letters concerning various topics about self-love, self-care, friendship, relationships, hurt, abuse/assault, feeling overwhelmed, anxiety, faith, positivity, breaking free, healing, growth and development, making choices, and more. I share some of my valley and mountaintop experiences to encourage you and let you know you are not alone, and you are victorious. This book includes scripture references that offer direction, hope, wisdom, and lessons. Additionally, special prayers are embedded throughout the text as I was led to do. As a bonus, I created a few exercises for self-inventory, key lessons, and fun.

    I desire that these letters and exercises will help you move in confidence knowing he will continue to supply all of your needs and grant you some desires of your heart according to his will.

When women support each other, incredible things happen.

Introduction

We do not know each other, but I can say with confidence we have walked in each other's shoes. Life has thrown you curveballs, people have sought to deter or destroy you, people have hurt you, women have tested your last nerve, and you have even doubted yourself. You have been tested in life and treated as less than human. Recognize you are a queen. Others have tried to overshadow you with darkness. Let your light shine. Life situations tried to flatten and bury you in the rubble. Yet, still, you rise. You thought you were weak until you heard a voice say you are strong and fearfully and wonderfully made. Through all of this, you are not totally convinced about the power of womanhood, sisterhood, and queendom.

This book will provoke your thoughts, provide tips and tools to live a life with clarity, challenge you to grow in self-love and love for others, and give you hope. I attest to this because the message is not about words to make you feel good. It is about reality and incidents I have experienced, people I know have experienced, and situations women can relate to in general. Real-life examples let the enemy know he cannot hold you captive with your story because it is meant to be shared. I have been abused, shunned, betrayed, faced with medical issues, and other challenges. Most importantly, I am an overcomer, surrounded by women who are victorious and have a relationship with my Redeemer. My life has not been without loss, pain and suffering, ridicule, shame, opportunities (open and closed doors), delays, failure, learned lessons, growth, and victories. I have been broke, busted, and disgusted, hungry, almost homeless, demoted, and betrayed. By the grace of God, I have been financially blessed. I am a homeowner, and have been promoted, elevated, and vindicated, to mention a few.

As you go through each letter and exercise, you will be challenged, connected, checked, self-assessed, encouraged, strengthened, and compelled to share. The queen in you will either be revealed or reminded to raise your crown.

Hurt from the One You Love

Dear Sis:

Why is your head hanging down? Why are you weeping? Where is your beautiful smile? I understand that the one you loved broke your heart. I understand that you have a heart of gold and gave more than you received. I understand that you just want to be valued, loved, and accepted. I understand that you question why your kindness is abused. I understand you feel that you care more than they do. I truly do. I want you to know that you are not alone. I want you to know your feelings are real, whether right, wrong, or indifferent. I also want you to know you will grow from this.

    Maybe it was your spouse, family member, a close friend, or other love who broke your heart. Perhaps who hurt you is irrelevant at the moment because you need to process it all (or get to the root of the matter). Today, I want you to know that the only person you can change is the reflection in the mirror. Yes, that is YOU! It is okay to hurt, shed a few tears, or have a sad face for a short while because these are human reactions to life happenings. Sis, it is time to deal with the hurt by acknowledging your feelings, and if safe and necessary, you can discuss your feelings with the love who hurt you.

    Come out of that fetal position waddled in grief; raise up and then stand tall like a queen. You are an amazing being and should walk with your head held high. You are a beautiful queen destined for greatness. Maybe you do not know this yet, but soon you will. I can say this because I have been hurt many times and in many ways. How I respond as a queen now is different.

Many years ago, I was pregnant at the age of seventeen by someone I thought was the love of my life. I told him I was pregnant. He asked if it was his. His insult cut deep. But that was not the hurt that brought me to my knees. He intended to break up with me right before I told him I was pregnant. He changed his mind only because he wanted to do what was "right." I thought it couldn't get any worse until I found out he confided with a mutual friend instead of sharing his mixed emotions with me. We were to be in this together.

By sharing this news, the next day our mutual friend felt the need to share my secret with our classmates during homeroom. The news spread like wildfire. Some teachers, administrators, and classmates began treating me differently. One classmate went so far as to lock the classroom door – the teacher had stepped away at the change of class – and would not let me in. I heard her yell through the closed door that they could not let me in because I was contagious. I heard laughter from beyond the classroom door. I was shunned, excluded, and felt I had been branded with a scarlet letter.

From there, I would go on to be shamed in the bathroom by a foreign language teacher, who questioned if my pregnancy was intentional to get a check (government assistance). That wounded me emotionally and mentally. What is more, I was moved from the front row of the choir to the back by my chorus teacher because the media was coming along with someone from the state capitol to hear us sing. I was considered an embarrassment. Once more, despite being an honor graduate, I was told that I could not sit on the front row because I was pregnant, and it was not a good look. I was not picture-perfect.

Add all of that coupled with the last straw, when the father of my baby – supposed love of my life – came home from college break, he began acting cold and distant. I asked why the cold shoulder and avoidance. While holding our baby in my arms, he angrily responded, "Because I do not want to be in a relationship with you anymore…I want to see other people." I was not enough. The lump in my throat… My world came crashing down. I felt I gave more than I got and received a lot of what I did not deserve from others. I felt like I was a leper no one wanted to touch or be around. My baby was a gift despite our irresponsible actions. What did we do to deserve such hurt? I fell into a stupor of self-loathing, and self-pity. Denial, anger, and depression seemed to clothe me, and the bed and couch became my coping mechanism for distress. I could not understand how people could be so malicious and cruel, particularly one who uttered words of love to me. Sis, I had forgotten who I was and my value in life. I had made myself inferior because of what people said and did to me. I gave them my power. It was because of my praying parents, a few loving family members, a couple of caring teachers, and a few supportive friends that I was able to rise from the ashes. I began to seek the Lord and encourage myself. I placed my focus on being the best me so that I could be a great example for my child. It was not easy, but when I shifted my focus to the plans the Lord laid out for my life, I was able to hold my head high and love myself, flaws and all.

 Sis, regardless of who hurt you, you are valued, you are loved, and you are destined for greatness. Reclaim your power and strength through prayer, meditation, and reading God's Word. Sing a song that lifts your spirit. Psalm 34:18 (NIV) tells us that the Lord is close to the brokenhearted and saves those who are crushed in spirit. Do not look to who hurt you to take away your brokenheartedness, because the Lord is our Savior. His sacrifices allow us to live victoriously even amid a storm. What can you learn about yourself in this season? Have you sought the Lord for direction? Have you acknowledged his direction? Examine these things and pick up your crown as you walk into your calling, your destiny.

I love you, beautiful queen. Remember, I am my sister's keeper.

Overlooked for a Job

Dear Sis:

I cannot begin to tell you the number of times I was overlooked for a position that I desired, felt more than qualified for, or pursued. I would feel hurt, disappointed, betrayed, and in some cases, bitter. I recall many years ago applying for a nursing audit position within an organization I worked and being told I was not qualified by the recruiter, only to be asked to train not one but two new hires in my role and responsibilities for my current position. They took the knowledge and tools shared to settle into their new jobs and evolve in their career. I could not understand why I was not qualified to apply or at least get an interview, but I was selected as a subject matter expert (SME) to train. I felt that the recruiter and manager did not see my value or wanted to keep me locked in because of my high performance. This was one of many instances over a period of fifteen plus years.

  One of the positions I later applied for, despite having subject matter expertise, a terminal degree in health administration, stellar performance, and my manager's recommendation, the hiring manager in the department went with another person outside the department who had not worked in that capacity. The difference this time was spiritual, mental, and emotional growth. I sought the Lord beforehand and affirmed that I only want what he has for me. If it were in his will for me to have that job, I would accept it; however, if it was not meant for me then I would still sing his praises. I follow the same mindset today.

  Sis, I briefly shared my story so you know that I have been where you are more than I desire to ponder on. I want you to know that there will be times when you feel deserving, whether in the workplace or elsewhere. You may feel defeated, hurt, disappointed, and disregarded. You may even feel like doing the minimum work required. You may shed tears. You may become angry and feel like lashing out. Take a deep pause, Sis, to do a self-reflection.

1) Who qualified you? Second Corinthians 3:5 (NLT) tells us that "It is not that we think we are qualified to do anything on our own. Our qualification comes from God." Your qualifications come from someone greater than you and are greater than what you see in front of you. You serve a higher purpose and wherever he places you is for his purpose, his glory, your good, and those who need to see your witness.

2) Who said that you are entitled to have that job? Sis, continue to be humble. Trust that God is in control. His Word tells us in Jeremiah 29:11 (NIV) "For I know the plans I have for you, declares the Lord, plans for welfare and not for evil, to give you a future and a hope." What he truly has for you is for you.

3) Did you hear the voice of the Lord direct you to make that move? Wait on the Lord, Sis. The Holy Word reminds us to "Be still before the Lord and wait patiently for him; do not fret when people succeed in their ways…" (Psalm 37:7 NIV).

4) Is that job truly what you want or need? Seek the Lord in all that you do. Ask the Lord to show you his ways and teach you his paths (Psalm 25:4 NIV).

5) Can anyone take something from you that God has ordained for you? Trust and believe that no one can take away what God has for you – not even the enemy can

approach you to test or harm you unless he gets permission from God. There is evidence in Job 1:6-22 (NIV), where Satan was allowed to test Job. Even in Luke 22:31 (NIV), there is a reference where the Lord tells Simon that Satan demanded to test them just as a farmer does when he sifts his wheat by separating the wheat from the husks. Likewise, Jesus was tested in the wilderness by Satan, but not before getting permission. These are just a few reference points that show despite the tests, trials, traps, or challenges placed before you, God has authorized the enemy because he has already equipped you to withstand the snares. All you must do is continue to seek him and follow his instructions. In 1 Corinthians 2:9 (GW), it states that, "No eye has seen, no ear has heard, and no mind has imagined what God has prepared for those who love him." He has already paved the way. He is omnipotent, omnipresent, omniscient, and a man of his word. There is no one like the almighty God, who works for those who wait for him (Isaiah 64:4 NIV).

Sis, though you may feel overlooked, you have been handpicked by God (1 Samuel 16 NIV). Find solace in the Word. Speak life and walk in authority in the name of Jesus. Be ready for what he has for you.

Church Hurt

Pause before you give up on church! The hurt you feel is real and your feelings matter. Church hurt is unlike any other because you expect more from church folks and leaders. You expect them to be above reproach and expect them to have actions that display love, compassion, and kindness. Luke 6:31 (NIV) tells us to do to others as we would have them do to us. You have probably asked, "How can Christians be so callous and judgmental?" Or you may have stated, "They are not Christians." You may have also said, "If that is what being a Christian means, then I do not want any part of it." These are natural responses. After all, each of us is human. Just know that we are not faultless or flawless. You cannot let someone's perceived antagonism push you away from your relationship with Christ or drive you away from where God has called you to be in that season. If anything, you should draw closer to the Lord, pray for them, and proceed as the Lord leads you.

    One of my most memorable church hurts experiences was during our first year of joining a new church away from our home state. We were excited to join this family-oriented church because it felt the most welcoming. It felt like a taste of home. The pastor was a remarkable preacher, teacher, and steward of God's Word. Members welcomed us and greeted us when we entered the Narthex and Sanctuary. I, of course, was nervous and guarded being two states away from home but was trying to adapt to our new church home. Within the first year of being a new church member, I was greeted with antagonism that wounded my soul. This is referred to as church hurt.

One Sunday, my husband and I dropped our kids off at children's church and then headed to the Sanctuary before service started. We slid in one of the middle section pews ready for praise and worship. Within a minute, a seasoned member walked up to the end of the pew and impolitely blurted out, "You are sitting in my seat and need to move!" I was appalled by such behavior and could not believe someone my senior and a Christian would behave so poorly.

You see, I am a southern woman from a small town where you practically know everyone. I had never been spoken to that way nor did any members (other than officers and honorary members of the church) have assigned seats. My soul felt crushed. I just laid my head on my husband's shoulder and cried. Not only were we new members, but we were in a new state and homesick. I felt the urge to stand up and walk out of the church, never to return. I needed a touch from home at that very moment. My husband urged me to not let people run me off, and he spoke wisdom and words of love to try and ease my mind.

In Holy Spirit fashion, a young woman with a kind face and dimpled smile approached. She apparently witnessed what transpired and asked us to join her in another pew. The young woman apologized for the seasoned woman's behavior and did her best to make us feel welcomed. She went on to say that there are no assigned seats, but some members are accustomed to sitting in specific pews seats, yet that does not give anyone the right to be mean. I felt hurt but encouraged by the young woman's kind gesture.

Moreover, I shared my story, Sis, so you could see that you are not alone. My husband kept teaching me along the way by reminding me "people are people," no matter if they are at church, the workplace, or in the streets. I had placed church folk and Christians on a pedestal because of the directives I read and believed from God's Holy Word. I had to change my mindset.

    Although antagonistic behavior is never okay, it is important to realize we have an Adamic nature, yielding to our flesh instead of what God has spoken. We sometimes ignore the Holy Spirit to do what makes our flesh feel good for that moment. Ephesians 4:31-32 (ESV) tells us to "Let all bitterness and wrath and anger and clamor and slander be put away from you, along with all malice. Be kind to one another, tenderhearted, forgiving one another, as God in Christ forgave you." We are reminded that we all fall short and sin, but we must strive to do what is right, forgive, and not hold on to hurt and anger.

    Sis, I stand next to you asking you to join me in "my pew seat," for you are not alone. You are welcome wherever God resides. You have unlimited seats and a fountain of love to draw from any time you need it. Wipe away those tears, soften your face with a smile, and release the hurt that holds you hostage. Follow God's many examples for how to live and respond to others. You are to be the vessel where God's light shines brightly, not only in the church but everywhere you go. Think about your actions when responding to others so that you do not make anyone feel any less than as you felt. Count this a life lesson and you will be all the better for it. You are a Queen! Rise, stand tall, and move forward.

Sexual Assault & Abuse

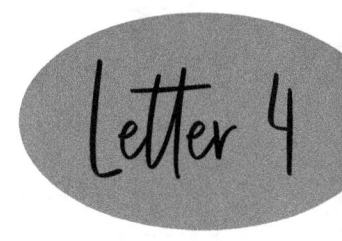

Dear Sis:

The unthinkable happened to you, and you held the hurt and pain inside. You could not bear the thought of what others would say and how they would react to you if they knew. You could not bear to think about it, let alone speak about it. You put on that perfect smile, cute outfit, and styled your hair when it was time to go to work and engage with people. All the while you were crying, cringing, and feeling unworthy and broken. You wondered what you may have done to cause him to hurt you like that. He stole a piece of you that day without any sense of remorse. You thought you knew him or were at least getting to know him. So many "should'ves, would'ves, and could'ves" crowd your mind. Even though time has passed since that moment, you are still holding onto the shackles of hurt, deceit, anger, and sadness.

    Sis, I want you to know that you are not alone. You are more than a conqueror (Romans 8:37 NIV). You are fearfully and wonderfully made (Psalm 139:14 NIV). First Peter 5:7 (NIV) tells us to give all our worries and cares to God, for he cares about us. Every tear you cried and every prayer you prayed, God heard you and will heal your broken heart (2 Kings 20:5 NIV). I encourage you to surrender it all today to him.

    Sis, I can encourage you to do so because I faced something similar many years ago and blamed myself. I felt ashamed and worthless. Sis, I even believed I had to remain in a relationship with this person because I was damaged goods. My thoughts were about protecting him, his reputation, and his freedom, but not about my safety and wellbeing. I was foolish to think that I had to be stuck and not allow myself to process and face what happened. I know it sounds crazy, but it is all true.

    Sis, I held that cancerous secret for years before I felt the courage to tell my mother, sister, and husband as a grown woman. What hurt just as much was the fact that the person who violated me was someone I knew, and he walked the earth as though nothing happened. Once, when we spoke, I reminded him of what he had done to me; he responded as though it was a casual experience and swept it under the rug. Yet, he knew how far to push me for fear that his perfect image would be crushed, and he would be exposed for all to see who he had become. Had it not been for a praying family, a strong support system, and the hand of God, I would have lost my mind and sight of who I was, but I had a purpose.

    Just as it was for me, you have God's Word and healing power. You also have support resources to help you process your feelings and get any additional help needed. Your friends, family, community, and I desire for you to be whole, happy, healthy, and free (#WHHF). Do not allow the predator's action to imprison you or seal your fate. Take the appropriate action and utilize positive coping mechanisms to not just survive but thrive. It is time to rise from the ashes like the beautiful Phoenix you are.

Prayer:
Now I pray, Lord, that you touch my Sis right now, from the crown of her head to the sole of her feet. Liberate her mind from clutter, confusion, self-loathing, anxiety, and thoughts of destruction. Wipe away every tear and all her fears. Wrap your loving arms around my Sis, Lord, and surround her with people who will uplift and help her during the road to restoration and beyond. Saturate her heart and mind with love, words of declaration, faith, and a fervent desire to do your will. Allow her

to turn her hurt into fuel to minister and encourage other sisters in need. Open doors that no man can shut, and close doors that need to be shut. Let the light of you, Lord, shine brightly through her so that others may be drawn to serve you. I ask all these things in your righteous and holy name, Christ Jesus, I pray. Amen.

Friendship

Dear Sis:

I am all for friendship, but I do not take it lightly or use it casually. What are your thoughts about this type of relationship? Do you call everyone a friend? Do you have both friends and acquaintances? I pose these questions because I want to share with you that not everyone is your friend. Depending on which dictionary you use, the word *friend* can mean 1) a person with whom one has a bond of mutual affection, 2) a member of a religious society of friends, 3) someone added to a list of contacts associated with social distance with a social networking website, or 4) to befriend someone. To me, a friend is someone you can lean on, who is supportive and encouraging, loving, honest and trustworthy, shares feeling of respect, and someone who puts the work in to maintain a healthy friendship. A friend can also be close enough like a sister.

Friendship is a gift, and it is not something someone should treat like a coat rack or musical chairs. Even though there is no greater friend like the Lord, there are special people who love and honor friendship with the heart of our Lord. Proverbs 17:17 (NIV) tells us that "a friend loves at all times." It is good and pleasant when friends dwell in unity (Psalm 133:1 NIV). Friends honor God's Word according to 1 Thessalonians 5:11 (NIV): "Encourage one another and build one another up, just as you are doing." Ecclesiastes 4:10 also reminds us to help one another up when one falls. These scriptures are some of the many nuggets of wisdom about friends and the look and feel of friendship.

It took life experiences for me to understand the types of friends or levels of friendship that exist. In fact, someone can be an acquaintance, peer, colleague, associate, dear friend, best friend, or sister-friend. There are probably more descriptors that may come to mind. What is important is that you understand the difference. How much time you invest, how much return on investment you receive, how much you chose to share, and how much you trust a person determines the friendship type or level.

Sis, I learned that people come into your life for a reason, season, or a lifetime. I understood how to be a friend but had to learn to let others in and not hold them to a high standard impossible for any man to reach or uphold. Some would say that as a Scorpio you must earn my trust, but once I declare you a friend or someone I care about, I am loyal to a fault. There must be mutual trust and respect, no fair-weather friendships.

I do not know where you are in your relationship with others, but I implore you to place value on friendship and not take it lightly. Know what you want in a friend and be that example. It is okay to have acquaintances; not everyone has to be your closest friend. You do not have to have a big circle of friends. Sis, it is okay to have a small, tight circle of friends who get who you are and compliment you as a friend.

Whatever you desire in a friendship, seek God and he will direct your path. He will surround you with people who are authentic and possess the key qualities of a friend as defined by God's Word. He will not only connect you to the right people but will help you be a better friend to others.

Decision-Making

Dear Sis:

You may be at a crossroads in your life or faced with an important decision that may have an immediate to long-term impact. You may be indecisive or feel overwhelmed. Before you attempt to make any decision, take a moment to pray about it. Do not move hastily. Wait on the Lord to provide you with clarity and direction. If you do not seek him in all that you do, you run the risk of chasing your tail, creating more delays, making poor decisions, and suffering the consequences.

    I can recall times when I made decisions and assumed God agreed with me. I did not seek him, nor did I seek wisdom from the elders in my life. Regretfully, my decisions either backfired or created a difficult road to get to when God had already laid the straight path. Likewise, some of my loved ones faced similar journeys because they failed to seek, listen, and then move according to God's will. The hardship we faced made us overly cautious at times until we found peace within. We had to forgive ourselves because God had already forgiven us. Instead of festering or sulking, we had to use those life lessons as growth opportunities. We are human and do not always get it right every time, but we must put our trust in the Lord. Even now we are seeking God for guidance in one decision or another.

    In Psalm 32:8 (NIV), the Word of God says, "I will instruct you and teach you in the way you should go; I will counsel you with my eye upon you." As the Father, he is wisdom, the provider, the guide, and the protector. He does not wish any harm to you. Whatever you lack in wisdom and understanding, he will provide the answer. Whenever you need him, he will be there.

Sis, you must be an active listener, for when he speaks you will know his voice and what decision to make. In Jeremiah 33:3, God tells us to, "Call to me and I will answer you and will tell you great and hidden things that you have not known." There are nuggets of wisdom on decision-making from the Old Testament to the New Testament in the Bible to pull from whenever you begin wavering and feeling weighed down about the 'next' in life.

Sis, just know whatever he guides you to do will bless you and work out for your good more than you can imagine. You may be able to testify to this from past decisions, but if this is new to you, try things his way. Enjoy the journey because he will blow your mind.

It's Not Too Late

Dear Sis:

Don't even try it! No excuses! It is not too late. I know you have been thinking about making moves to begin that new project, complete your education, change your career, start a family, birth a new business, or start living again. Wherever you stand at this moment, either allow the Lord to interrupt your hurry or allow him to move you from procrastination to expedition. Accept the gift of time to pursue your dreams and use the talents you have been given. In 1 Peter 4:10 (NASB), it states, "As each one has received a special gift, employ it in serving one another as good stewards of the manifold grace of God." "Thanks be to God for his indescribable gift!" (2 Corinthians 9:15 NASB)Even though you may have taken a different exit from the directions provided, you can get back on the guided path here and now. You know what you need to do. You have heard the calling. You have seen the vision. You have even felt a touch of what is to come. Look no further for confirmation, Sis, because it is not too late!

In the 1960s, my mom (affectionately called Patsy) was forced to drop out of high school because she was pregnant with my oldest sister (deceased) Pam. My mom and dad soon married because they loved each other and that was the expectation during that time. Due to her new priorities, my mom could not finish night school. She had to take care of her family first. She would later accept the call to minister God's Word as an evangelist. Over the years, she continued to sacrifice for her family and to do the Lord's work. Even in doing what she loved, there was a tug on her heart to finish what she started all those years ago. My mom thought she was too old and that ship had sailed. With family support and a nudge from God, my mom soon realized it was not too late. In the early 1980s, she would go on to earn her diploma. She was proud, and we certainly were proud of her as well. Yet, God was not finished.

By the mid-1990s, my mom's job with United Technologies Automotive, Inc. (UTA) ended. The manufacturing company permanently closed in our community. An opportunity arose through a partnership with the local Workforce Center and UTA to help the employees find jobs, go to college, or both. My mom felt encouraged to further her education. She was reminded that it was not too late. Nothing was holding her back. She went on to complete her associate degree in business office management, and by the early part of the new millennium, she earned her Bachelor in Business Management degree. By the time she finished her associate degree, she landed a great job as the office manager for the local Sheriff's Office. She would go on to become a community development counselor with the Marlboro County Community Development Corporation. Her education was an extension of her ministry, and she was able to help a great number of people with their finances and buying their first home. People spoke highly of her even after she passed in 2016. Regardless of what was going on or the many challenges, it was never too late for her to move forward in the direction God gave her.

Sis, I shared all of this to encourage you and to remind you that it is never too late. Remind yourself that "I can do all things through Christ who strengthens me" (Philippians 4:13 NKJV). Honor the Lord with your actions and move forward as he has directed you.

Prayer

Dear Heavenly Father, I first give you thanks for who you are and all that you continue to do in our lives. I ask for a special blessing and clear direction for my queen sister and your child. Remind her that all things are possible through you and let her know she is not alone. You have given us the Holy Spirit to guide, comfort, nudge, correct, remind, and advocate for us. Anoint her afresh and revive that which is in her as well as those things you've birthed in her all those years ago. Show up and show out, Lord. Let her know that it is never too late to pursue dreams, turn over a new leaf, and achieve goals. Everything that she does in your name, Lord, will accomplish what you intended it to do. Surround her with people who will uplift her and hold her accountable. Let her words and actions reflect you so that others may seek to serve you. I ask that you touch my queen sister's family, finances, ministry, mental health, and physical health like only you can. This is my prayer in the only name that matters, in Jesus's name I pray. Amen.

Self-Esteem

Dear Sis:

Has your self-esteem always been low or has life happenings dampened it? Perhaps you were not the most popular or outgoing person growing up. Maybe you were told you are not pretty enough, smart enough, thick enough, tall enough, or not enough in general. Maybe you looked in the mirror and just did not like what you saw. I want you to know that you are not alone and that you are an amazing being. In case you did not know, you were uniquely created. I am reminded that as early as my mother's womb, I was fearfully and wonderfully made, and the Lord's workmanship is marvelous (Psalm 139:14). In every complexity of our being, the Lord had his hands in it all. He created a masterpiece that is to be a mere reflection of who he is and stands for even beyond this world. He created us in love, and for that alone we should love ourselves and be confident that what he created is worthy and valued (Genesis 1:26-27 NIV).

    No man can truly appreciate the masterpiece unless he had his hands in it; nor can a man truly understand the intricate details in which our minds and bodies are woven. Therefore, we must look to the Lord for reassurance, wisdom, and confidence in who we are and what purpose we serve.

    Sis, I encourage you to affirm that you are more than the thoughts of any being. You are more than what the eyes can see. You are more than any stereotype or grouping that man has defined. It is in him that we live and have our being (Acts 17:28). We cannot escape him because we are nothing without him. Our reverence should be in him, the master of all that we do, think, or breathe. He has us in the palm of his hand. Allow him to live in you and to fill your mind and heart with those things that are uplifting, of peace, and spoken in love and truth. No longer look to please others and neglect yourself. Increase your belief in the Lord and the promises he has made, and stay away from self-sabotage mentally and in action. Strengthen your spiritual connection with the Lord. Preserve you, the masterpiece, by practicing self-love, highlighting positive self-image by affirming his Holy Word, and employing the resilience he has given you.

I leave you with words of wisdom spoken by Joyce Myer: "God has equipped you to handle difficult things. Sis, he has already planted the seeds of discipline and self-control inside you. You just have to water those seeds with his Word to make them grow!"

Love the Skin You're In

Dear Sis:

This may be cliché, but it is true – you are beautiful! It does not matter the shade, texture, or race you are assigned. Love the skin you are in! So what if they said you were not light enough, dark enough, black enough, brown enough, or white enough! Sis, replace your crown because the skin you are in is like the eighth wonder. In Song of Solomon 4:7 (MSG), it speaks of your beauty from head to toe. How can you argue against the Word? God has already spoken.

You are not oblivious to the woes of the world, the words of man, and the actions of hate and destruction that surround us, but you must remind yourself who and whose you are. Sis, you are the child of the Most High God. Be thankful for the flaws and imperfections of your skin.

Do not tear down another woman based on her skin. If it is jealousy you feel, rebuke yourself and seek the Lord for that unconditional love. Just like the rainbow, every color is beautiful. Just like paint on a canvas, each color is beautiful. More importantly, the way the painter blends the primary colors to create an array of other colors extols the masterpiece. Every shade is a blend of God's creativity and perfect will, and for that we should always be in awe. "Do nothing out of rivalry or conceit, but in humility consider others as more important than yourselves" (Philippians 2:3 CSB).

Just as important, when we come together as a body, we are as a botanical garden of flowers, beautiful in all our ways. We do not blend, we compliment! We do not shade, we amaze!

Therefore, Sis, let the light of the Lord shine through you by standing boldly in the skin you are in. Know that the Lord created you with a purpose and for his glory, just like he created other beautiful queens. Embrace his creation and love the skin you are in because you are a limited edition.

Accentuate the Positive

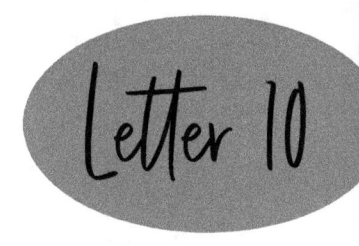

After a few minutes of listening to an encouraging song or spoken words of wisdom, you cannot help but be moved. While listening to a praise and worship song, you cannot help but thank God for every blessing and all he continues to do for you and others you know and love. Even looking at a piece of art can inspire you. There are beautiful and inspirational things all around us to encourage us to accentuate the positive even in the lowly moments.

If you reflect on your life, you will find that you have overcome so many adversities in life. People all around you (and maybe yourself) are facing mountains, but this ministry moment through song reminds you to give him praise for every mountain in your way. He has and will continue to bring you over and see you through.

Sis, your test will turn into a testimony that will not only bless you but others around you. Some people sit afar observing how to manage a situation or person, however, you may not be aware. They see how you accentuate the positive despite any challenges or adversity you may experience. This in turn gives them hope and encouragement.

Even before the COVID-19 pandemic, there has been so much negative energy, actions and hate, selfishness, deceit, and anti-this and that, but this heightened climate has moved to an all-time high in my lifetime. It can be discouraging, draining, stressful, disheartening, isolating, and more. Sis, it is imperative that we individually pull ourselves together and collectively uplift and lend a helping hand to others. We are better together!

1. We must refuse defeat, naysayers, disbelief, and negative energy.
2. We must remind ourselves of the many mountains we have overcome individually and collectively as people.
3. We must remember who parted the Red Sea so we could get to the other side, away from our antagonists and oppressors.
4. We must remember how God multiplied our little where we could nourish ourselves and pay our bills.
5. We must remember those before us who have been to the mountaintop and shared the goodness of the Lord.
6. We must remember when we almost gave up and he sent a ram in the bush. God provides.
7. We must remember when we could not lead anymore or utter more words of encouragement, God sent us an Aaron and a Hur to prop us up in a time of need.

It is when we remember these things, we can say hallelujah; for this Lord, we give you praise!

Death & Grief

Dear Sis: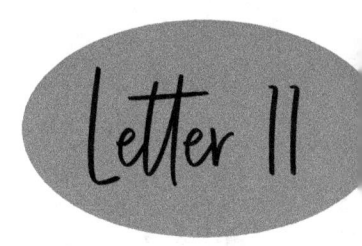

Death is all around us and is inevitable. Death comes in many forms, such as the loss of someone or something dear. Perhaps you or someone you know is facing the death of a loved one and you feel broken like all hope is gone. As a survivor of losing my mom and other close relatives and friends, you *can* thrive and begin to enjoy life again. Even though that special person is no longer present, you can hold on to beautiful memories and personal belongings. You may find comfort in knowing that "the LORD is close to the brokenhearted and saves those who are crushed in spirit" (Psalm 34:18 AMP). Even Paul declared in 1 Thessalonians 4:13-14 (NIV), "Brothers and sisters, we do not want you to be uninformed about those who sleep in death, so that you do not grieve like the rest of mankind, who have no hope. For we believe that Jesus died and rose again, and so we believe that God will bring with Jesus those who have fallen asleep in him." Although you may grieve, you are still blessed by the Lord because he embraces you as his child (Matthew 5:4), provides comfort, and reminds you that you can lean on him.

    In various scriptures, the Holy Word reminds us not to fear because Father God gives us strength and holds us steady and safely in his arms (Isaiah 41:10 MSG). This does not mean you have to hold in your grief or pretend it does not exist. Sis, you are to grieve, but not be hopeless since you have the Comforter. Leverage healthy resources to help you heal. Take the necessary time needed to process your grief. Do not let anyone tell you how to feel. Utilize your support group as needed. Acknowledge your feelings. Do not lose sight of the power of prayer, the Word, and time.

Sis, you know the end of the story because of what is written throughout the Bible, particularly the book of Revelation. Going through the grieving process will help you overcome without losing fond memories of your loved one or sight of who you are in the Lord.

Join me in prayer.
Lord, touch my sister, her family, and her loved ones like only you can. Death is all around and is inevitable. Although death and grief are natural, we are of flesh and remain in need of your hand in every facet of our lives. Send your comfort, and shower down your peace and love. Clear out the clutters in the corners of our minds and allow your mighty touch of understanding to invade every crevice and space. Fill our hearts with more hope and remind us of the evidence of your fulfilled promises that we may expand our faith in you. We ask all these things in your son Jesus Christ's name, we pray. Amen.

Toot Your Horn

Letter 12

Dear Sis:

I see you making moves to better yourself. You did that!
Do not be bashful or downplay your accomplishments or worth. You are a remarkable, intelligent, innovative, and resilient woman.

Do not worry about what others think. Naysayers will always play their role. There may be some cheerleaders in your corner, and that is okay. The most important thing is that you acknowledge your progress and successes. You are a winner!

Do not wait for others to praise you so that you can feel honored or recognized. Those things are nice but may not happen when you expect them. Instead, toot your own horn! You did the work, put in the time and effort, made sacrifices, and saw things through from beginning to end. These are things of which you should be proud.

I worked with a very pleasant and professional young lady (I will refer to her as Mary) who took pride in her work and helping other team members. Mary was modest and rather coy about kudos received for her hard work, collaborative efforts, and innovative systems and processes. She was also timid when it came to completing her self-evaluations for performance reviews. Mary shared she felt uncomfortable speaking to her contributions and rating her performance appropriately. For example, Mary received positive feedback for outstanding customer service, but she rated herself as average and above average on established goals. Exceeds was an option she did not fathom could be used to describe her. Mary did not rate herself as exceeds for any goal despite having stellar performance. Fortunately, I had the opportunity to mentor Mary and to bring attention to her high performance within the team and with management at different levels. As a result, she was assigned special projects, received awards for outstanding performance, and was also promoted to a lead role. Mary came to realize that it was quite acceptable to toot your own horn. She was blessed with gifts and talents to help others and did her best in all that she touched. In doing so, she glorified God.

Therefore, Sis, do not sit on your gifts and talents. Do not miss out on blessings because you are too bashful to toot your own horn. There are times when you do not have to utter a word but be aware that in other times it is important to celebrate yourself. You must allow others to celebrate you as well. Remember you are a shining star, so let your light shine!

Proverbs 16:3 (MSG) states, "Put GOD in charge of your work, then what you've planned will take place."

They Won't Support Me

Letter 13

Dear Sis:

You or someone you know may have said this at least once or twice: "They won't support me." There is some truth to this. Some will support you while others will not. Let us be more specific. You may have a new business endeavor and are somewhat positive and hopeful that people you know (or even love) will support you as a customer. That is a common thought, and it may be the expectation. Unfortunately, not everyone you know (and love) will support your business. Some will support you in words of encouragement. Some will lift you up a prayer. Some will make a purchase. Then there are those who will ignore you, discount you, and expect something for free.

Do not lose focus on your brand, mission, vision, and target audience. Never limit your audience. Promote your business because others are sitting and watching quietly to see how you fare. You have piqued their interest. They desire to invest or support, but you must be assertive and dedicated. They want to see how far you go with your stick-to-itiveness before they invest or make a move. If you are willing to put in the time, others are willing to support you at the right moment.

My grandmother used to say those who need to be there will be there. I found this to be true through my journey and business endeavors. Supporters will come from different walks of life and unsuspecting people. Sis, your purpose is greater than your immediate circle. The Lord called you to go beyond and stretch what he has provided. Choose to look beyond what you see and remember "Hakuna Matata" (do not worry about it).

Psalm 34:10 (NKJV) reminds us that "the young lions suffer want and hunger; but those who see the Lord lack no good thing." The Holy Word also tells us in 2 Corinthians 9:8 (NLT), "And God will generously provide all you need. Then you will always have everything you need and plenty left over to share with others." The Message translation makes it plain: "God can pour on the blessings in astonishing ways so that you are ready for anything and everything, more than just ready to do what needs to be done." Sis, do not despise those who do not support you. Shake the dust off your feet and keep it moving. Follow as God leads you in your business. Think of your business as an extension of your ministry. Do not forget to be a blessing to others, and in all you do give God the glory.

"They" may not support you, but there is a whole world of people who will. The people who identify with you and the services your business provides are the ones you target. Stretch your reach and be prepared for the blessings to come.

Please join me in prayer.
Gracious Father, thank you for allowing us to be entrepreneurs and establish our businesses. Thank you for turning a dream into reality. We thank you for the vision and the path forward. We bless you for the naysayers and the faith builders. We bless you even more for your grace and mercy over our lives and others. Continue to whisper words of encouragement and wisdom. Help us to be obedient and good stewards. Help us to be a vessel to bless others. Let your light shine brightly through us and offer hope to those in need. Bless our businesses, finances, tithes, and offerings in good measure, pressed down, shaken together, and running over. We love you and give you all the honor and glory. It is in Jesus's name we pray. Amen.

Now You Know You Were Wrong!

Letter 14

Dear Sis:

I know you did not just do what I think you did to her! I know you did not say what I heard you say to her! Did you just cuss her out for no apparent reason? Did you just tell her that lie? Did you just shame her in front of everyone? Sis, why? You know you were wrong! There are better methods you could have used to say how you feel or get your point across. As women, we do not have to be abrasive or savage-like with one another. Our words do not have to cut like a two-edged sword. Our actions do not need to humiliate or defile others while losing a part of ourselves in the process. You do not always have to have the last say or prove you are right. Please understand I do not get it right all the time.

    Sis, I have learned and continue to learn when to speak, when not to speak, what to say, how to say it, and how to respond in general. I have learned when I am wrong to acknowledge it and sincerely apologize. I am learning how to channel my feelings into something positive without losing sight of the root of the matter. Day by day, I seek to employ lessons learned. Even the COVID-19 pandemic, tragic events, and other life happenings over the past two years have taught me to think more before I respond, and to choose my words more carefully. What many saw as isolation during the pandemic for more than a year, I saw it as a time of breakthrough and revelation. I found more peace and self-awareness. More importantly, I grew closer to the Lord. Although I have more work to do and must rely on the Holy Spirit to keep me in check, I can see the growth from all my experiences. My words now have more seasoning, and my expressions are less judgmental.

In James 1:19 (ESV), we are reminded that every person should be quick to hear, slow to speak, and slow to anger. The words that flow from our mouths should always be gracious, pleasant, and savory, so that we will know how to answer each question others ask of us (Colossians 4:6 NIV). How many people do you know who would not appreciate admirable behavior?

When we step out of character or respond with ugliness, we must acknowledge and ask for forgiveness from those offended. This includes forgiving yourself, because you not only hurt others, but you also assault a little bit of your humanity and your temple. Sis, remember to display the fruit of the Spirit, including love, joy, peace, patience, kindness, goodness, faithfulness, gentleness, and self-control (Galatians 5:22 NIV). As followers of Christ, we do not follow selfish and thoughtless behaviors (Galatians 5:23 NIV). We must own it!

Just know growth is a journey, and you must be a willing participant. I believe in you, but God believes in you even more. Allow the light of the Lord to shine brightly through you.

No to Negative Energy

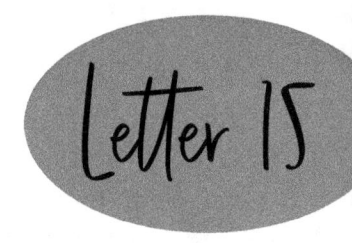

Dear Sis:

I do not know about you, but I say "NO" to negative energy. I can be negative all by myself (if I so choose) and do not need anyone to join the bandwagon. Why do I say NO? Quite frankly, it is exhausting! I strive daily to stay positive and avoid negativity where at all possible. If nothing else, life experiences have taught me that I should thrive and enjoy all that the Lord has given me.

- Life is too short and precious to fight battles that belong to the Lord.
- Life is too short and precious to try to change people to do better.
- Life is too short to put your life in the hands of others.
- Life challenges and temptations are ever so present to trust that people will always be ethical and apply moral values.
- Life's history tells us that old habits die hard.
- Life has shown us that sometimes we must stand alone.
- Life has shown us that with the help of the Lord we can set the tone wherever we go.

Since we have an Adamic nature, it would be foolish to continue thinking that people will not let you down. People will try to discourage you. People will try to hurt you because of the goodness and the 'Son Light' that they see in you. James 3:16 (ESV) tells us, "For where jealousy and selfish ambition exist, there will be disorder and every vile practice."

Proverbs 6:34 (ESV) further confirms that jealousy produces fury, and when someone is relentlessly envious, they will seek to harm or wound you, whether spiritually, physically, mentally, emotionally, or socially.

Yet, it is vital to find solace in the Word of the Lord. "Do not be conformed to this world, but be transformed by the renewal of your mind, that by testing you may discern what is the will of God, what is good and acceptable and perfect" (Romans 12:2 ESV). Despite how others perceive or treat you, avoid actions of rivalry or conceit, but be humble and elevate others as God would have you to do (Philippians 2:3 ESV). Live by example and let your positive energy flow.

You can pray for the naysayers and negative conduits from afar. Yes, I said pray for them – not because I am the authority, but because the Lord says to do so. "Do good to those who hate you, bless those who curse you, pray for those who abuse you" (Luke 6:27–28 ESV). Let this resonate with you.

Sis, if the Word does not make it plain enough for you, consider the world of science. There are protons, neutrons, and electrons in an atom. Protons are positively charged and dwell in the nucleus (core/center). Due to the weight of a proton (P), it has a significant impact and aid in the identity of an atom. Neutrons are not charged but dwell in the same place as protons. Neutrons are known to share space with protons with ease. Even if a neutron was negatively charged, it would draw to the proton for a positive charge. As you may have guessed, electrons are negatively charged and lurk around the nucleus. Both the protons and electrons can shape the atom's identity.

In this context, the atom is God and his nucleus is Jesus Christ. The proton represents the Holy Spirit, the neutron represents us, and the electron represents the enemy (name unworthy to mention). To create a positive atmosphere that represents God our Savior, we (the neutrons) must faithfully reside and lean towards the Holy Spirit (protons). In doing so, we become reflections of the love and identity of the Son who conquered deaths for our sins. However, if we connect with the electron (the enemy) circling and waiting for an opportunity, we become exposed or even engrossed in negative energy. We become more of a reflection of the enemy.

Although there will be negativity in one form or another, surround yourself with positivity. Go to that secret place that empowers you, makes you smile, encourages you and others, gives you peace, and shifts the atmosphere.

In summary, it is up to you what atmosphere you choose. As for me, I say "NO" to negative energy and encourage you to shift your atmosphere into something positive, energizing, and profoundly resembling our Lord and Savior.

I leave you with this quote by Laliah Gifty Akita: *It is better to dwell on the beautiful things in life than the negative.*

Health Care Treasures

Dear Sis:

As a seasoned health care professional and educator, I cannot stress enough the importance of taking care of your health. Let me first acknowledge there are many people who are uninsured or underinsured. According to Cohen et al. (2019), the National Health Interview Survey 2019 showed approximately 33 million (approximately 10 percent) persons of all ages were uninsured at the time of the interview.[1] By the second half of 2019, more than 35 million persons of all ages (11 percent) were uninsured (Cohen et al., 2019).[1] This is two million more than the first half of the year. I cannot help but wonder what the statistics look like for 2020 and 2021 given the COVID-19 pandemic. While individuals rally and push for better legislation for healthcare for all, alternate solutions should be developed to meet the needs of this population of people.

Considering this disparity with health insurance coverage, those with private and public insurance should count their blessings. It irks me when people with health insurance coverage (particularly full coverage) do not treasure their health care benefits. It vexes me when people get sick or symptomatic enough where it warrants medical, mental/behavioral health, or dental care refuse to utilize their health care benefits (treasures) to get the care they need. I think about people who have lost their lives because they had little to no health insurance coverage to pay for prescriptions, procedures, or other necessary treatments. It is heartbreaking. When they sought medical or other healthcare treatment they were turned away or given subpar care because money played a factor. Some people have faced near-death situations while others have died because of a lack of or refusal to be compliant.

I could go on and on with my soapbox, but I will get right to the point. Sis, if you or someone you know does not have the health insurance coverage needed, please tap into all resources available to you and seek guidance from resourceful people. If you or someone you know has health insurance coverage and does not use it for preventative, maintenance, or urgent/acute care services, I encourage you (and those you know) to take advantage of the health care treasures you have. Take care of your body and mind because you only get one life.

What a Difference a Smile Makes

Believe in true beauty and the power of a loving smile because it can reveal the ultimate magic of life. — Debasish Mridha

I must be honest with you: I love everything about my smile. I like a full genuine smile. It makes me feel good, and I love the way it influences others to return the favor with their smile. I am most proud of my smile because it is my mother's smile. It is infectious and feels like home.

Sis, pause a minute to smile and think about how it projects to others and makes you feel. A smile warms the heart even when you do not feel up to your best. It softens a hard face and soothes a person's demeanor.

If you search the Internet, you will find forty-five to fifty or more songs across various genres with the word smile in the title. Some of the popular songs you may find include:

- When You are Smiling (The Whole World Smiles with You) by Louis Armstrong in 1929
- Smile by Nat King Cole in 1954
- Sara Smile by Hill & Oats in 1976
- I Love Your Smile by Shanice in 1991
- A Wink and a Smile by Harry Connick Jr. in 1993
- Just to See You Smile by Tim McGraw in 1997
- U Smile by Justin Bieber in 2010
- I Smile by Kirk Franklin in 2011
- Smile by WizKid featuring H.E.R. in 2020
- Smile by Katy Perry in 2020

If you listen to some of these songs, you will likely find yourself smiling and singing along.

There are studies about smiling and laughter. Author Betty Ann Heggie (2019) echoes that smiling is contagious, so much so that it can shape and mold us as early as infancy.[2] "So called "mirror neurons" (important in early human development) allow babies to mimic facial and emotional responses and fire in response to sensory input (Heggie, 2019, para 3b).[2] Heggie (2019) compares the mimicked response to yawns to that of a smile.[2] I can attest to this. Whenever I greet someone with a smile, they smile back (even though they were not smiling beforehand). A smile creates a chain reaction. I could have a sour disposition with my husband, but when he graces my present with his beautiful and loving smile, it melts my heart and makes me smile. Sis, who would not like that feeling?

If you are not convinced, do your research. You will find a plethora of information about the difference a smile makes.

I hope that you will use your smile as a tool to spread sunshine to all those you encounter. Consider the Word of God: "A cheerful heart is a good medicine; But a crushed spirit dries up bones" (Proverbs 17:22 ESV).

The Power of Laughter

Dear Sis:

I just finished a belly laugh and it felt good. Sometimes, I read commentary just to get a good laugh. Sometimes, I watch TV for comic relief. Other times, I chat with family and friends, reminiscing about old stories and making new memories with bloops and blunders. All of this is for therapeutic laughter. It energizes me, calms my nerves, and helps me not be uptight and unbothered. Granted, there is a time and place for everything, but I find there are more moments to enjoy laughter.

There are testimonials and literature all around us that speak to the power of laughter. According to the Mayo Clinic (May Clinic Staff, 2019, April 5), laughter has short-term and long-term benefits.[3] Did you know that laughter can stimulate your organs, activate and relieve your response to stress, and ease tension short-term (Mayo Clinic Staff, 2019, April 5)? As a nurse, I am aware, but it does not stop me from reminding myself to laugh more. The long-term benefits are just as amazing because laughter has shown improvement in one's immune system, pain relief, increase personal satisfaction, and mood (Mayo Clinic Staff, 2019, April 5). As a disclaimer, laughter is harmless so long as you are not doing so at the expense of other people.

Laughter comes with other benefits in engaging with others. Considering the physical and mental health benefits highlighted, you will likely feel more comfortable and motivated to build and strengthen relationships. Laughter can inspire you to collaborate with others, as well as improve your conflict management skills.

Sis, laughter is for people of all ages. Author Betty Ann Heggie (2019) reported findings that "children laugh about 400 times a day, but adults on average laugh only about 15 times" (para. 2).[2] This a huge gap! If you are one of those adults barely laughing, then you have some homework to do. You are not alone in this. We, as adults, need to up the ante with more laughter. Heggie (2019) encourages the reader to be like a bee with our laughter, using it to pollinate flowers (spread to others) and bring them to life (personal wellbeing, relationships, interactions).[2]

Now that we have covered the power of laughter, I implore you to take some time each day to enjoy appropriately healthy laughter. You should have an idea of what makes you laugh and can tap into those resources. The more you practice laughter, the more you will likely find other things that make you laugh. Give it a try. You have nothing to lose, but everything to gain from the experience.

I'm Not Superwoman

As I sat in the chair getting my hair groomed, my eyes and mind drifted off to a place beyond the windows in front of me. I was in a low place, searching for a reason for my demise, a season of suffering and persecution. I felt the flat affect of my face and the poor posturing as I drifted farther beyond the view in front of me. What did I do to deserve this? Just when things were turning around for me and my family, there it was waiting for me…the "valley experience!"

October 2014 is a point in time I will never forget. Suited in my shero suit, I entered the workplace with a prayer in my heart and praise on my lips declaring that I will make it through this stressful environment again today. Let us see what needs to be tackled today because someone has to take the reins and I am that someone today. Little did I know that this shero would fall cripple to the stressors of life. It was around 9:30 in the morning and no other leaders in sight but me…people coming from every direction with their needs…in the blink of an eye, the room began spinning, my throat began tightening, my chest started pounding, a rush of emotions emerged, tears began to well up, and everything seemed to be in slow motion…I could not believe what was happening. Yes, I fell captive to the dreaded panic and anxiety attack combo! How did I get here? The answer is simple! I took on a role that was only designed for one person who was given authority to be all things at all times and in all places to all people! It was not a superhero that I became, but it was a substitute savior!

In the initial days of my valley experience, time was spent regulating my level of anxiety, increasing my hours of sleep, and clearing my mind from the cares of work, home, and church life. Yes, it was exactly what the doctor prescribed. It was also an appointed time by the Lord so that he could speak to me without any obstacles of confusion and disruption.

It was in this recovery mode that God began to speak to me about where I was and where I needed to be in life. I had to realize that the burdens or weights of others were not mine to bear. I was neither a superwoman nor a savior. It was time for me to re-prioritize and focus on the most important things in life.

Sis, so many women try to take on so much and carry weight on their shoulders whether they realize it. People will treat you like a trashcan pouring all their garbage in because you can be counted on to take care of things. People seek you for guidance or other needs when it is convenient for them, but do not take time to get to know you and see how they can help or at least carry their load. Some people will ride on your coattails for as long as they can. You must realize you are not a superwoman. Sis, we must stop loading our plates! There is only one to whom we should cast our cares and that is the Lord! Praise belongs to the Lord, to God our Savior, who bears our burdens each day (Psalm 68:19). Sis, now take off your cape because you are not a superwoman. Be the disciple he has called you to be, serving as a witness of his love, power, and directives for our lives. Point those who are burdened to him who is the rock, the master of the sea, and the breath that we breathe. He is far greater than superman and superwomen and has no limits to what he can and will do for each of us. The Lord is indestructible and knowing that he has the world in his hands tells us that he can carry every burden.

Let's pray.

Gracious Father, we bless you for showing us our limitations and reminding us that we can and must depend on you in every aspect of our lives. We thank you for your abounding grace and mercy and unwavering love. We come before you surrendering our cares to your hands. Forgive us for trying to be something or someone we are not. We humbly ask that you give us a peaceful mind, body, and spirit. Shower down your wisdom and knowledge as a guide for our daily walk in life. Help us to keep our mind on you and seek you in all that we do. Place your protective hedge around us. Let your word transform us as armor so that we can stand against the trick of the enemy. Remind us we are victorious through Christ Jesus. We love you and we bless your holy and righteous name. Amen.

I am Happy for Her but Envious

Letter 20

Dear Sis:

Maybe your colleague received the promotion you wanted or thought you earned. Maybe your friend purchased a home you dreamed of having one day. Perhaps your family member is 'on the come up' financially and able to make money moves. Perhaps your neighbor is a socialite who seems to have it all, including a huge circle of friends. Maybe your church members appear to have a seamless marriage or relationship you so desire to have with your love. You may have mixed feelings where you are happy for them all, yet you are also envious. There is no need to be envious of someone.

What is being envious? The dictionary defines *envious* as a feeling of discontented or resentful longing aroused by someone else's possessions, qualities, or luck. Envious thoughts and feelings are roadblocks. Instead of being envious, we should celebrate with others and trust and believe that if God did it for them, he can do it for us. The Word tells us not to covet what others have in numerous scriptures. We must learn to be content in whatever circumstance we are in, whether we have a little or a lot. Additionally, we should take care of what we have. Doing these things does not mean that you cannot go before the Lord to petition him for some of the desires of your heart. Although he can do all things, some desires may not be in his will. We must remember that his grace is enough and that he does his best work in our weakest moments (2 Corinthians 12:9 NIV).

Sis, I would encourage you to do a self-inventory to understand your feelings and actions when you see others blessed in areas of life that you desire to have. Be real with yourself and be accountable. A self-inventory can bring revelation and healing. If you find that you are an envious person, seek God for wisdom on how to work through that negative response. You will not lack anything good as you continue to seek the Lord. Whatever blessings he has for you are for you.

Prayer

Dear Heavenly Father, I come to you on behalf of this beautiful queen, first thanking you for your grace and mercy. Thank you for the blessings whether big or small that you have given her. Lord, as she takes inventory of her life and innermost feelings, help this queen to see those things that are holding her back from a closer walk with you. Let her know that you have a greater purpose and plans for her life. Help her to be content and trust in your Word. Let her know that someone's blessing is not a threat to all that you desire for her. Help her to study your Word and trust that you have everything in control. Let her know that she can seek you anytime and anyplace. Guide her thoughts and actions. I pray that as you continue to bless her that she pays it forward and blesses others. I ask these things in the name of Jesus. Amen.

Peeling Off Layers

Dear Sis:

Just when I thought I was making progress along comes another task, another situation, another issue, another obstacle, another him, another her, another challenge! Last week I passed the test and here I am again in a similar situation, and what did I do – I failed my test. Ugh! How frustrating! How disappointing! Once again, I realize my weakness as a human being and more so my walk with Christ. I cannot do anything on my own accord. I am like an onion that must be peeled to get to the core of who I am. I am an onion waiting to bloom, but before I do, some things must occur.

Let me tell you how I got to be so tough on the outside. As a toddler, the doctors counted me out and others looked at my frailty in my sickened state. Up came my first layer of skin. I am a fighter, and no one should count me out. In comparison to my sister and brother next to me, I was not cute enough or light enough. I was the ugly one… the homely looking one…the servant one. Up came another layer because no one recognized my beauty. As I continued to blossom as a child, I was the crybaby and frail one, the weak one, the soft-hearted one…just not tough enough. There went another protective layer of skin. The onion continued to grow a thicker skin for protection…protection of the heart…the core.

By the time my teenage years came, I was the good girl, too good to make a mistake or be a failure. I was placed on a pedestal and the price of failure was too costly to pay. Again, another layer of tough skin went up. By my senior year, I was pregnant with my first child, and now, the perfect image, scholarly student, award-winning cheerleader, popular in-crowd, and the do-right young lady became shameful, talked about, and finger pointed at. Yes, she had it…that disease, that taboo to be shunned. Again, another tough layer was added. The skin of the onion grew thicker – year after year, situation after situation – for protection. The thicker the skin got, the less feelings there were towards people, even those who were closest to me. The journey took me to one last layer of skin after a miscarriage, financial burden, and loss of home and car…there was no more room for additional layers without strangling the core or the heart of what remained of me.

The growth of thicker layers continued until I transitioned to Virginia with my family. I told God I wanted to get to know him more for myself and not live off the relationship that my family had with him. It was so familiar, but was my relationship the way it had to be? God spoke that it was time to strengthen my core, open my heart, lift my eyes, and spread my wings to fly. It was indeed time to peel off the layers so that others could benefit from his Glory, his masterpiece, and his work in me. I was meant to be his blooming onion. As he began to peel off each layer, I began to weep. He spoke, "Weeping may endure for a night, but joy is on its way…your morning is near. Everything that you went through was for my Glory…count it all joy. I was with you every step of the way. Just as it is spoken in my Word, I will never leave you nor forsake you. I was pruning you and getting you ready for greater things. You are my child, a treasure that others deemed worthless, tarnished, and frail, but my child you are seasoned to the core, you are free to serve and witness to others."

"Tell them your story – how I saved you, molded you, and gave you a tender heart to love and pray for my people. I allowed your body to be attacked so that the enemy could see that you are not easily broken. I allowed you to be the least likely so that others could see how I can open doors that no man can shut. I allowed you to feel what many are suffering so that you could be a witness that I am able and have all power. I am the way, the truth, and the life. You lost stuff, but you gained more spiritually in me. You asked for more of me, and I had to get rid of the obstacles that were binding you. Greater work I have for you, and you were spared as a toddler because greater was coming."

"You were never meant to be in the in-crowd or the one to fit in because you were called to deliver the word to my people. You were called for my purpose and set aside to give me the glory. It can feel lonely, but I am always with you. I will always provide the Comforter and a way for you to witness to my people. If you are mixed in with the crowd, then you cannot hear my voice. My beautiful child, no need to keep any layers, you are protected by my Word and sacrifice! I have paid it all! Bloom on my child, and let the core, which is a portion of me, be tasted by those you encounter. They, too, can begin to peel off layers because I am their protector and send my Comforter!"

Sis, you have read my testimony. So, I say to you today, at this moment and in this hour, you are to release those things that stifle, strain, choke, squeeze, abuse, or bind you! Allow yourself to listen to the Father who created you with purpose. Be open to the direction he provides so that you can help others in need. Sis, it is time to blossom by peeling off the layers. Other queen sisters have need of the gifts within you.

Lonely in the Crowd

Dear Sis:

I look around and see that every crevice and four walls in the room are crowded, but all I feel is an empty place and a feeling of loneliness. I hear the crowd chatting away, but they do not hear me. I see who they are, but they do not recognize me, except when they need what I can offer.

Therefore, I close my eyes and go to the secret place where there is a sweet whisper, peace, encouragement, love, hope, comfort, and my presence and heart's desires are acknowledged. The Word and the sweet melodies of God's promises soothe me in the crevices and innermost walls of my soul. Yet, I soon recognize that I cannot stay in this sweet place. I must dwell in a world, for at least a while, that crushes and crumbles you in one moment, and then caresses and cherishes you in the next. Contrariness and inconsistencies are what I see. But I realize that for me to be free and live in peace in this season, I must continue to fill my mind with thoughts of his love. I must fill my heart with melodies from the angels above. I must fill my soul with the Comforter that makes everything alright. Moreover, I must recognize that I will never be alone when he is beside me, behind me, in front of me, on the sides of me, and all around me! When the crowd rejects me, he will always carry me and lead me to a place of refuge (Psalm 18:2 NIV). This is not just my story, but it is yours as well. Seek refuge in him, for he can take you from the valley to the highest mountain. He can make you visible to the world because of the light that shines from you. He can take your gifts and talents and use them to set others free. Hence, lonely you may need to be for a while, but when you go to the sweet, sweet place and feel his presence, you will not seek refuge in the crowd. Your destination is beyond the confines of the room and its four walls. Sis, you are just being separated to lead the crowd.

Eternal Security: Rooted in Christ

Dear Sis:

The Holy Bible provides many instances and examples of being rooted in Christ. To be *rooted* is to be embedded, entrenched, and surrounded. In essence, to be rooted in Christ is the same as saying your life revolves around him. Christ is our Lord, and his Word is implanted in our hearts, spoken from our mouths, and exemplified by our actions. Just as the Earth uses the Sun as a power source, we need Christ (God's only begotten Son) as our power source. The more rooted we are in him, the stronger and steadier we are in facing life's toils and snares.

As I thought about being rooted in Christ, I was reminded of a tree. A tree is a unique symbolism of the Godhead and Christians. Think about it. A tree has several parts, but there are only a few essential parts that we must identify. Keep in mind that the physical part that we consider to be the top of the tree is not the highest point in the hierarchy. The pinnacle point of a tree is the root. The root represents God, as it is the foundation or base that serves as an anchor and aids in absorption. In other words, anchor suggests that God is permanent or everlasting; just as absorption means that God soaks up the troubles of the world.

The next essential part of a tree is the trunk. The trunk represents Jesus. Experts consider this part to be the most important part of the tree. The trunk is a stabilizer and provides the greatest support. It also is a great resource for timber, serving many purposes and of great value. Jesus served God's purpose by showing how to love your enemies, living a holy life, caring for the helpless, and many more amorous actions. Just as the trunk is the middle portion (or go-between) of the tree, Jesus is the mediator for the petition of our sins who shed his blood so that we may have everlasting life. As the trunk is used for timber, Jesus was the ultimate sacrifice, nailed to the cross, brutally beaten, hung his head, and died. But it did not stop there! Just as the trunk, he stood tall and strong, being raised from the dead.

The third essential part of a tree is the branch. The branch represents the Holy Spirit, in that it reaches out, providing a connection between Christ and man. The branch can be both large and small, serving whatever purpose Christ deems necessary. Just like the branch, the Holy Spirit moves in many directions. It can be uplifting, long-lasting, comforting, and straightforward. Once a branch is removed, it can be used as a walking apparatus or even a rod. The Holy Spirit guides your footsteps by leading you in the right direction and convicting you of any wrongdoing.

The last essential part of a tree is the leaf. A leaf is a flat, thin, expanded organ that represents man, better yet, disciples of Christ. As with a leaf, we are fragile beings who must go through various stages in life, and at some point, we must die. Our earthly and eternal life is dependent upon the personal connection or relationship with Christ. We must understand that we are like leaves blowing in the wind. The only source of eternal life and security rests solely in our roots. We must recognize who God is, believe that he sent his Son Christ Jesus to die for our sins, and he provides us with the Comforter in the time of trouble. Stay rooted in Christ by reading God's Word, fasting, praying, and ministering to others.

Matthew 12:33 (NIV) states, "Make a tree good and its fruit will be good or make a tree bad and its fruit will be bad, for a tree is recognized by its fruit."

Sis, we know that Christ is the good tree, bears good fruit, and any other fruit is not of him. What fruit do you bear?

Don't Try Me; Try Jesus!

Dear Sis:

Some people will make every effort to test your goodness and kindness. They will test you to no end, hoping to bring out that ugly personality. They do not want you to go high as they stoop lowly to wound you. Let them know: Don't try me; try Jesus! It may sound strange, but there is a method to this response. The Lord has declared he is our refuge and redeemer. Every time your adversaries and enemies rise up against you, they will stumble and fall (Psalm 27:1-2 NIV). He also reminds us that whenever there is trouble, he will keep us safe in his protection, in his secret shelter. He will hide you and lift you up on a rock (Psalm 27:5 NIV). Safely up on a rock keeps us from the adversaries and enemies' grasps. Not to mention that Jesus is the rock of our salvation, meaning our escape. When they act against you, they pick a battle with our big brother Jesus. (I pity the fool!)

Sis, adversaries and enemies tried to break him who is unbreakable. People laughed at the words that flowed from his mouth but had no idea of his omniscience. In true ignorance, they did not think his sermons would reach the masses but had no clue about his omnipresence. The antagonists sought to vilify him but did not know he is worthy to be praised. Crowds saw weakness due to his bruised body but did not see his omnipotence. They sought to torture his body but had no idea of his deity. They also tried to bury him but did not recognize he is the resurrection and the life. At every turn, the adversaries and enemies tried Jesus. In case they do not know, he is the Son of the Living God, Christ, Almighty,

Author of Life, Deliverer, Gate, Great Shepherd, Hope of Glory, and Immanuel.

After you tell them his story, let them know this: When you try me, you try Jesus. It is better to let me introduce you to him than to seek him in your defeat. If you have come to battle me, my Savior has already won and made me victorious. If you contemplate ways to hinder me, my Lord has already made plans to prosper and not to hurt me. As a bonus, he has given me hope and a blessed future I can count on. You can try your best to turn others against me. It will not matter because he is greater than the whole world against me. His love is unwavering.

Sis, let them know with certainty, don't try you; try Jesus!

Build Your Faith Muscles

Dear Sis:

Several years ago, I came across an article titled "10 Best Tips on How to Build Muscle" by Rachel Cosgrove in the Men's Journal.[4] As I was studying about faith, God gave me a Bible study called "10 Ways to Build Faith Muscles." I am not sure where you are in your faith walk but wanted to share this with you.

Spiritual fitness is just as important as physical fitness. There are several things you can do to build your faith muscles, and I have defined them as follows:

- **ACTION 1**: The first thing you must do is FUEL UP by reading the Bible to get a sense of how you should live and walk daily. Begin with the book of Genesis and start feeding yourself with at least one chapter each day. Aim to reach at least 30-45 minutes a day in feeding on GOD's Word to reduce any weight that you have.

- **ACTION 2**: The second thing you must do is LIMIT CARDIO. Stop running from anything that haunts you. Stand strong by praying in sprint intervals, up to 30 minutes three times a day.

- **ACTION 3**: The third thing is to DO LESS. Do less complaining and instead increase your level of praise. As one of the gospel songs chants: Turn your pressure into praise and give him Glory every day! This will help you gain more faith muscles.

- **ACTION 4**: The fourth thing to do is USE FULL BODY WORKOUTS or a SPLIT ROUTINE. To get the best results from your workout, you must meditate on GOD's Word and put on the Armor of GOD – the right equipment. This includes the following:
    - The Helmet of Salvation (Ephesians 6:17 NIV)
    - The Breastplate of Righteousness (Ephesians 6:14 NIV)
    - The Belt of Truth (Ephesians 6:14 NIV)
    - The Shield of Faith (Ephesians 6:16 NIV)
    - The Sword of the Spirit (Ephesians 6:17 NIV)
    - Gospel of Peace (Ephesians 6:15 NIV)

- **ACTION 5**: The fifth thing to do is STRETCH. Increase your faith muscles by stretching them not only with a smaller obstacle but also with bigger obstacles. Partner with prayer warriors and massage your muscles with anointing oil to help keep you flexible, prevent injury, and improve recovery between workouts (called trials and tribulations).

- **ACTION 6**: The sixth thing to do is EAT REGULARLY: Just like your natural body desires regular, healthy meals (five to six small meals) daily, so does your spiritual body. You cannot feast (one big dump or buffet of his Word) and think that will last for the day. No, you must intentionally and purposefully eat reasonable portions and snack on his Word (whether through scriptures, song, praise, dance, etc.) at a minimum of five to six times each day. As long as good-quality fuel (the Word) keeps coming into your spiritual body, particularly protein (strength) and carbs (energy), you will have the calories to build faith muscle and the metabolism boost (the ability or gift) to lose fat (dead weight).

- **ACTION 7:** The seventh thing to do is CHANGE EVERYTHING: Every four to six weeks, you need to alter some part of your routine, whether it is the number or length of time you fast, the amount of time you spend with God, the way you exercise your faith, or any other praise and worship variable.

- **ACTION 8:** The eighth thing to do is TRAIN THE WHOLE BODY. The more spiritual muscles you involve (from head to toe), either in one exercise (stepping out on faith) or training session (test of faith), the greater anointing and breakthrough you get from training. This stimulates faith muscles all day long. Hitting each muscle group with roughly the same measurement of faith exercise will ensure balanced training, allowing you to grow quickly and safely, avoiding injuries, and preserving flexibility (able to move around, over, under, and through obstacles).

- **ACTION 9:** The ninth thing to do is DRINK SUPPLEMENTS. Support your workout (stepping out on faith – faith in action) with nourishment, starting with a high protein (studying his Word) and carbohydrate (prayer) meal about an hour beforehand. Mix up a protein shake (Old and New Testament with praise and worship) and sip that throughout your workout (stepping out on Faith – faith in action). After a workout, finish the drink and mix a new one for every workout that follows.

- **ACTION 10:** The tenth and final thing to do is RECOVER. The ideal amount of sleep is seven to eight hours per night. This allows time for your body and mind to be at rest so that the Holy Spirit can speak to you, your body can recuperate, and restore your fuel to get up and journey another day for God's sake.

Sis, while you are building your faith muscles, add a little anthem music to get you pumped up. "Go Get It" by Mary Mary is a great warm-up song to get you started. When you feel like quitting because it is too hard, listen to "Survivor." For the cool down of your workout listen to "You're Bigger" by Jekalyn Carr. Build a playlist of other empowering songs that will carry you through your workout each day. Watch how strong your faith muscles become as you commit to the workout plan.

They Can't Stop My Shine

Dear Sis:

The enemy cannot stand light and seeks to surround you with darkness by using other people and situations. It is because of that power of darkness that they will try to stop your shine. According to Ephesians 6:12, "For our struggle is not against flesh and blood, but against the rulers, against the authorities, against the powers of this dark world and against the spiritual forces of evil in the heavenly realms." In reading God's Word and facing tests and trials in life, we already know that the enemy will consistently do what he does 24/7. We must stay prayed up and listen to the Holy Spirit. God has fully equipped us to withstand the enemy, according to Ephesians 6:10-18 (NIV):

Armor of God

1. Belt of Truth: Stand firmly in truth, which is the Word of God, as it is your foundation.

2. Breast Place of Righteousness: Be obedient to God's Word and let your actions be pleasing in his sight.

3. Feet Prepared with the Gospel of Peace: The Lord is the Prince of Peace and our firm foundation, whom we should follow as the example for how we live our lives. We should walk in peace because he has paved the way and freed us from sin.

4. Shield of Faith: No matter what it looks like, stand on the Word of God by activating your faith. It is faith that saved us and it is faith that will sustain us. "For we live by faith, not by sight" (2 Corinthians 5:7 NIV). Shield your heart, mind, body, and soul with absolute faith in the Almighty God.

5. Helmet of Salvation: If you have not done so, I encourage you to accept Christ as your Lord and Savior. Believe that he was born, died for our sins, and raised from the dead, then you are saved (Romans 10:9 NIV). That is what salvation is all about — delivered from our sins.

    If you are already saved, then remind yourself about the ultimate sacrifice the Lord made for our sins and how he continues to be our shield of protection. He gives us grace and mercy. He freely gives us what we do not deserve, and as an added benefit, he graces us with kindness instead of punishing us when we deserve it. As Jesus walked in flesh, he was faultless and showed us how we should walk and respond to God's commandments in life. Never forget that.

6. Sword of the Spirit: This is the Word of God, and you should keep it hidden in your heart as a daily recharge. The Word protects you, guides you in discipleship, sustains you, comforts you, feeds you, and is a free open source for everyone and everything in life. It is filled with instructions and a road map for life. It is the ultimate offensive weapon created by God and known to man. Isaiah 54:17 (MEV) confirms, "No weapon formed against you shall prosper, and every tongue which rises against you in judgment you shall condemn. This is the heritage of the servants of the Lord, and their righteousness is from Me," says the Lord."Sis, he

is your light and your salvation. Whom shall you fear? The Lord is the refuge and fortress of your life. Whom shall you dread? When the wicked came against you to eat up your flesh, your adversaries, and your enemies, they stumbled and fell (Psalm 27:1-2 AMP). As we walk in peace and assurance from the Lord, you will continue to have victory over the enemy, and they will continue to stumble and fall.

In understanding just a few small but powerful nuggets of God's Word, you are fully equipped. Whenever the enemy tries to overshadow you with darkness, the "Light of Son" will shine brightly through you. With God at the center of everything, you are unstoppable. The rays of "Son Light" are beyond the brightest sun and have infinite boundaries. Therefore, Sis, know that as you stay connected to God, they cannot stop your shine.

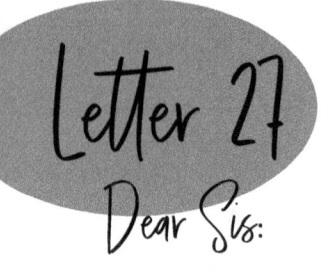

Don't be Scared; Lean into It

What are you afraid of? What is holding you back? You have a purpose, and there are things placed on your heart and engrained in your mind for you to execute. You are gifted to share and bless others. Lean into it.

Maybe you are scared to take the next step with the ministry or business birthed in you. Maybe you are scared to apply for that job because you do not feel qualified. Perhaps you are scared to walk away from a position, relationship, or home you have known for so long. Perhaps you have been scared to tackle that new project, make that new purchase, or further your education after so much time has passed. Whatever it is, listen to the voice of God and lean into it.

Sis, so what if you made moves before and things did not work out the way you wanted them to. You are not a quitter. You are one who perseveres. You are not defeated. You are more than a conqueror. You are not alone. You are surrounded by love, and God has you in the palm of his hand. You are not cursed or unworthy. You are favored by God, and he continues to extend his grace and mercy. You are not hopeless. You are filled with hope and nothing less than Jesus's blood and righteousness. You are not weak. You are strong and mighty in the Lord.

These reasons alone are reminders to overcome your fear and lean into what God has called you to do. Words of wisdom from Proverbs 16:9 (NIV) remind us that although our heart plans our way, the Lord is the director of our steps. He is omniscient (all-knowing) and there is no need to doubt or fear what lies ahead. As you continue to seek him, he will remove obstacles that block our path (Proverbs 3:6 NIV). Author Margaret Fishback Powers and other authors at different times are known for writing a powerful poem titled "Footprints in the Sand." The poetic and enlightening words remind us that even though we may see only one set of footprints as we walk through some of the scariest times in our lives, the Lord is still with us, carrying us every step of the way.

Sis, there are powerful scriptures that speak to the omnipotent, omniscient, and omnipresent attributes of God that should stay close to your heart.

- He will always be with you. (Deuteronomy 31:18 NIV)

- God works all things according to his plans for the good of us who love him and are called according to his purpose. (Romans 8:28 NIV)

- No need to be afraid because the Lord has delivered us. We are victorious because of him, and we belong to him. (Isaiah 43:1 NIV)

- God's perfect love removes all fear. (1 John 4:18 NIV)

- The Lord is our rock, fortress, and our deliverer. He is our place of safety, strong tower, provides us with his armor, and is impenetrable. (Psalm 18:2 NIV)

As a believer, he has given us irrefutable evidence of who he is and whose we are for eternity. As fear attempts to creep in, resist and rebuke that spirit of the enemy. You are empowered and more than a conqueror. Sis, whatever he has placed on you to do, do not be afraid; lean into it. Watch how he blesses you for your obedience and yields fruits of your labor beyond what you imagined.

Unexpected Love

I do not know where you are in your life with love or whether you are finding love in the wrong places and people. I can tell you that love can come unexpectedly and from the least expected person. I know from personal experience.

  A little more than two decades ago, I was traveling to the nearest big city with my boyfriend looking to trade in my sports utility vehicle (SUV). We ended up at a used car dealership first where I spoke to a young salesman. After several minutes of discussion about what vehicle I was interested in purchasing, the salesman referred me to a new car dealership in the next city. In giving his instructions, the salesman told me to ask for a salesman named Craig Burch. He assured me that the new car salesman could help me. We left and headed to the next city.

  About thirty minutes later, my boyfriend and I made it to the new car dealership. I asked for Craig Burch and introduced myself to him as he walked up to me. As I explained to him what I was looking for, my boyfriend began looking at cars as well. After the preliminary paperwork was completed, I was asked to come back the next day. My boyfriend and I did just that. I was very chatty as my usual self while my boyfriend sat back. He was not very observant and that is what peaked Craig's attention.

  Craig made a profit that day by selling both me and my boyfriend a car. He told us he would contact us whenever our license plates were ready. Within a couple of weeks and a few calls later, my boyfriend's tags were ready. We picked up my boyfriend's license plate from the dealership. My license plate still was not ready that day. Craig informed me that he would call when my license plate arrived. I was beyond ready for my license plate to be placed on the front and rear of my new vehicle. I followed up later to see why it was taking so long. Craig explained that the paperwork was backed up. That seemed odd to me, especially knowing my boyfriend had his license plate. Sis, little did I know that Craig had a plan.

    Shortly after that day, Craig called to say my license plate was not ready, but he needed me to sign some more paperwork. He stated he would come to my job which was about forty-five minutes away. A question mark fired off in my head. Craig showed up smiling with gleaming eyes. My colleagues were checking him out as he conversed with me. He told me that as soon as my license plate was ready, he would drop it off. I could not believe a license plate takes that long. My radar went off. He found reasons to not have my license plate ready until the last minute when my paper tags were about to expire. The waiting period was filled with calls checking on the status of my license plate. All the while he was buying time as it would be later revealed. Craig knew I was not pleased with all the delays. He volunteered to deliver them to my home, which was forty-five minutes away. I thought to myself who delivers license plates to someone's house. Then I justified it by saying that is the least he could do for such a long wait.

    Sis, it just so happened he delivered my license plate one evening on his day off with his youngest son in the back of his car looking and staring. My boyfriend was there and stayed in the house while I was speaking to Craig about my license plate. The conversation continued as Craig sparked discussion. Craig made it a point to say he would not have his woman outside talking to a man if it was him. (I failed to mention that Mr. Burch was not my type, but his observations of me, my boyfriend, and how others thought he would be a catch for me sparked his interest and motivated him to pursue.) What he did not know was I was tired of the same old drama with my boyfriend.

Craig continued to make follow-up calls to see if I was enjoying my car. He would later send me a dozen roses to my job. What was a woman to do but take notice? The roses were a sweet and unexpected gesture that I was not accustomed to. Getting tired of the staled relationship with my boyfriend and puzzled by the interesting and sweet gestures from Craig, I had to walk away from the dead-end relationship and focus on myself. Lauren Hill's album inspired me to break free from the drama. No more settling.

Despite my best efforts, Craig Burch was not catching the hint either. I wondered why Craig was pursuing me so. He told me that he wanted to show me how a young woman should be treated and let him be himself and treat me as a man should. I, of course, entertained the thought. Eventually, I told Mr. Persistent Craig we could be friends and go from there. I invited him to church thinking he would fail the test. He proved me wrong. He showed up pleasantly eager to worship. Craig took me to dinner and opened doors. He later drove me to his home city (sixty minutes away) to meet his family. I was not used to that with the guys I had dated in the past.

Sis, Craig made sure he was around every day just about from that point on. He got close to my family and they rallied for him. For Mother's Day that year, he treated me and paid to get my hair done. He even drove me to the salon and sat there until I was done. I seriously thought to myself, *what is up with this man? Is this for real?* My dad was and still is a good man but I just never experienced such wooing in my younger years in relationships. Craig even surprised me with a mini shopping spree, buying my mom and himself something. At first, I refused to get anything because I was suspicious of his motives and did not want him to think that would open any doors for him. I was miss independent. (Boy, was I dumb then, Sis. Can I get a do-over on shopping?) I questioned what was happening. *Who does all this stuff? Is this a joke?* Despite my initial resistance, my mom was a happy shopper. I ultimately picked a couple of things to appease everyone.

Craig and I continued to spend time together over the next few weeks. Before I knew it, he said he loved me and then asked me to marry him. Yet again, I thought to myself, *What? You do not really know me nor I you.* He had the diamond ring and all. Lord knows I was confused. I had a couple of long relationships and did not know them as I thought, and now, here is a real man (older than me by several years) whom I barely know, and he is doing all the things that a woman dreams of at such a young age (thoughts of a fairytale). I exclaimed to myself, *This is crazy! I met you in February and it is now at the end of May. You want to get married?!* While he was on one knee, I said, "Ah hold on, I need to talk to my mom." I had to run to my parents' house next door. I told my mom this was all happening too fast, and I did not even know how I felt. I had just gotten out of a three-year relationship. I asked my mom what I should do because the idea of marriage after knowing each other for more than three months was crazy. My mom said, "You can learn to love a good man." *Say what?* After a real conversation with my mom, I still felt overwhelmed and went back to my house and told Craig I was not ready yet. He decided to make it a promise ring and I was okay with that. I could breathe again. No man had expressed love for me other than my dad and brothers. It had always been me giving more than the guys I dated.

After another week of being together every day, Craig and I went riding miles away enjoying each other's company. One day the light bulb went off: This man loves you, and so what you have not known him long or it was unexpected. I had prayed to God all those years back about this and the gift was staring me in the face. Did I love him? I did not know at that time, but I recognized the gift. I told Craig, "Let's do it. I will marry you." He lit up with that lovely smile. He could not wait to tell everybody. He asked my dad for approval. He assured his family I was who he wanted and that we were not rushing into things. I remember him praying as we held hands: "God if this is not right, make us right for one another. This is forever." He was willing to sacrifice many things to be with me. That meant the world to me.

We wanted to go to the courthouse, but his family wanted a wedding. We decided to honor their request and we planned a wedding at his parents' house near Charleston, SC. It was a garden wedding. I must say that the words "I love you" never came from my mouth until the day before we got married. We were riding in his car to do some last-minute errands. I had previously thought this was truly happening, and I did not know if I loved him or not until that day. Despite my uncertain feelings, Craig was at peace with that because he had enough love and faith for both of us.

We wedded on Sunday, July 25, 1999, in the late afternoon. I was so nervous. It was a beautiful day that took a turn for the worse. Unfortunately, my dad fell deathly ill a few hours after walking me down the aisle. He ended up in the intensive care unit (ICU). Despite it being our honeymoon time, my beautiful and loving husband, Craig, showed just what kind of man he truly was. He took charge of the family supporting us as well as my mom and sister as we stood by my dad. Thankfully and prayerfully, he survived and recovered from the illness over six months. Our honeymoon was delayed for a year, but that was not important. He was my rock and cared for my parents as a birth child would.

Sis, my husband is not perfect, but he is an imperfect, unique gift molded just for me. He can be broke and still have riches to share with me. More than two decades later, we remain in love and strong in our marriage. Who knew that the man who sold me and my then-boyfriend cars back in February 1999 would end up being my husband five months later?

Sis, recognize the gift that God has for you and stop looking for a false perception of love. What God gifts to you is perfect! I praise God for Craig and give him all the glory for this unexpected love!

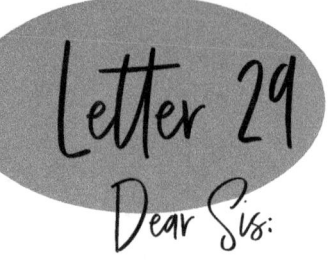

Sister Circle

Dear Sis:

Are you spending more time in the house and not connecting with people outside the house? If you are, then you need to make a change. Everyone should have a sister circle. We were not put on earth to be on an island by ourselves. Sure, you may be comfortable in your own space, but life is not about being complacent in isolation. We need human connection. Whether you are in a relationship or not, it is important to have social development.

COVID-19 forced nations of people to quarantine and be confined to home or measured spaces for more than a year. It was a scary time, and many people felt alone or were alone and craved human connection. Others were able to cope because they had friends to call on whether by phone or video conferencing apps. These resources helped people to not only survive the pandemic but to thrive.

Although I had my immediate family at home, I needed more than their faces and presence. Thankfully, I had a circle of friends to call on and share fun moments with. My circle of friends made me laugh and let me cry my feelings out. As a sister circle, we enjoyed movie nights and book club meetings. We held video conferencing meetings just to chat and chew. One of my favorite things that happened was when we played games. Although I had a circle of friends before the COVID-19 pandemic, spending virtual time with my circle of friends made a world of difference in my life.

Having a circle of friends helped me step out of my comfort zone and feel comfortable becoming a praise dancer more than thirteen years ago. They helped me open up where I could allow honesty and trustworthy people to get close to me. As a circle of friends, we prayed together and continue to do so to this day.

I read a scholarly article by Neal-Barnett et. al., (2011) titled "Sister Circles as a Culturally Relevant Intervention for Anxious African American Women."[5] The purpose of this study was to "investigate the utility of employing an intervention predicated on the support of other Black women" (Neal-Barnett et. al., 2011, p. 266).[5] The study revealed how important it was for a black woman to have a support system with other black women. The authors further concluded that "sister circles come with many benefits, serving as a support group that builds upon existing friendships, fictive kin networks, and the sense of community found among African American females" (Neal-Barnett et. al., 2011, p. 266).[5] This study resonates with me because my sister circle helped me through a rough patch when I was diagnosed with anxiety disorder, followed by a serious car accident a few months after that, and then the death of my mom almost a year later.

Sis, not everyone is for you. Some may be on your side for a while until they are not. Check your circle. Declutter your circle of those who do not add to the sistership and surround yourself with a circle of women who support you in the good and bad times, and you support them as well. Remember that no woman is an island. Get connected and stay connected to your sister circle.

You Can't Stop My Praise

Dear Sis:

Do you find people stirring the pot, staring at you, or getting annoyed because you love to praise the Lord or because of how you praise the Lord? If so, you are not alone. If, by chance, you are one of those people who respond in such a negative manner, maybe you should do a self-evaluation for why you feel indifferent. I praise the Lord the way I do, like many others, because of his goodness, grace, and mercy. He has not only been there for me in the best of times, but he was (and remains) with me in the worst of times. When the doctors told my parents I would not live past the age of five, the Lord showed he was the great physician and timekeeper of life. Every prayer my family prayed over my life, the Lord honored those prayers. Decades later I am still standing.

When I got pregnant in my senior year in high school and people ridiculed, shamed, and shunned me, the Lord gave me strength and courage. He surrounded me with love and support from people you would least expect, in addition to my family. When I was sexually assaulted, it was the Word of God, prayers of the righteous, and the Comforter to remove the shame and not go into a deep state of depression. When I gave up on love, the Lord honored my prayers and those of my parents. He sent my Boaz and blessed me with a blended family.

Once again, the Lord made a way when my dad was on his deathbed – he sent his healing power. When I faced pregnancy complications with my youngest child, he surrounded me with a caring and skilled medical team and a praying husband and family members. My son is alive and well.

When I suffered from depression with my last pregnancy that ended in miscarriage, he gave me the strength to go to work each day so that I could help take care of my family. I remained depressed for some time afterward. The Lord touched my parents' hearts and they agreed for my mom to come to live with me and my family for a year hundreds of miles away from our home state. Even when the antagonists in the workplace and church rose against me, he protected me, gave me a stronger voice, and elevated me in the presence of naysayers. For every stumbling block that came my way while working towards my educational goals, he made them steppingstones. Even when I thought I couldn't take any more and my beautiful mom passed away at the beginning of the year several years ago, the Lord carried me every step of the way. Where I once felt broken almost to no repair, he restored my joy and directed me on how to thrive in my new normal. The Lord gave me the drive to press my way and I completed several degrees and certifications, including my doctorate in health administration.

Yes, Sis, he made a way and keeps making a way. I could testify and sing praises of his immeasurable love for me and others I know. Every time the enemy or life happenings sought to quiet and destroy me, the Lord showed up and showed out. His love and kindness, omnipotence, omniscience, and omnipresence elevated my praise.

Psalm 95 is all about worshipping and honoring the Lord for being the rock of our salvation (he saved us) and the King of all kings. I praise him even more because he is unchanging (Hebrews 13:8 NIV). Isaiah 25:1 (ESV) acknowledges that the Lord is our God, and we should exalt him. We should praise the name of the Lord because of all the wonderful things he has done and continues to do in our lives. Deuteronomy 31:6 (MSG) is the icing on the cake: "Be strong. Take courage. Don't be intimidated. Don't give them a second thought because God, your God, is striding ahead of you. He's right there with you. He won't let you down; he won't leave you."

It is for the above-mentioned reasons why no one can stop my praise!

Prayer

Lord, I give you honor and glory and praise you for all that you continue to do in our lives. I come before you to intercede on behalf of my sister. If anything is hindering her praise, release it from her or show her what she must do to set herself free. Let her not be concerned with what others are thinking or doing. Help her to keep her eyes on you as you continue to provide direction for her life. Fill her cup and continue to extend your grace and mercy. Let her share her testimonies as you would have her to do so that other people can be blessed. I pray a special blessing over her household, health and wellbeing, finances, and the journey ahead. I ask all these things in the matchless name of Jesus, I pray. Amen.

I Love You, But Sometimes You Pluck My Nerves!

Dear Sis:

I do not know who this applies to in your life, but sometimes the person you love gets on your last nerve. The feeling may be mutual. Maybe you know this, maybe you do not. At this moment it is not about them but all about your thoughts and feelings. By now you may have thought of at least one to two people who pluck your nerves the most, yet you still love them.

    I would be the first person to admit that there are people I love who pluck my nerves. Most of them know it whether right or wrong. However, some are oblivious. Some people can handle your truth about what frustrates you about what that loved one says or does. Some cannot handle the hard truth; therefore, you must find other ways to work around that.

    When I was a child growing up with three other siblings (younger sister and two older brothers) in the home, my nerves were tested more than I could count. One of my brothers loved to tease us. He was what we called "pickyfied." He lived to annoy his siblings. My other brother liked to tease and bully us, take a mile instead of the inch given, and thought he was the best-looking person in the house. He was what we called the "Satan-seed" and the "sneaky one." Then there was my younger sister who used her baby status to the fullest to wrap my parents around her finger. She loved to get my brothers in trouble and sit back with a devious smile. (She was adorable though.) Most of the time she did this after my brothers annoyed her. She would also fake tears to gain sympathy and blame her siblings for something. We called her the "sneaky one" too. I was considered the "goody two-shoes (do-gooder)." Anytime they used their menacing crafts, they would pluck my nerves. I would call them out on it and at times take appropriate actions.

Fast forward to adulthood, and a whole new level of plucking nerves was revealed. As an adult, I have greater expectations of people. The older I get, I find that my tolerance level is not what it was when I was in my twenties or thirties. There are people I love who are very close to me but pluck my nerves. Again, I am sure the feeling is mutual. I love my husband and children dearly, but there are times I have to let them know my nerve is hanging on its last thread with them.

I used to choke down my feelings, but as I evolved into adulthood, I became more vocal about them. I wanted them to be clear. In recent years, I have learned to do a self-assessment and awareness check of each of my family members. Although I am very expressive, I take moments to pause, breathe deeply, and go to a positive headspace when I feel they are plucking my nerves. Sometimes I communicate my annoyance and other times I decide that it is not worth the frustration or negative energy. Sometimes I require 'me time.'

The same is true for other loved ones in my life. You would think social cues would make a difference, but that is not always the case for some people. In fact, many times that is not the case.

In strengthening my relationship with Christ and personal and professional growth, I can rise above others' nerve plucking more than before. Do not get me wrong, sometimes they need to know, but in all seriousness, how I manage annoyance, pettiness, and negative energy is what matters the most. I desire to be whole, happy, healthy, and free (#WHHF) from annoyances that seek to distract me or wound me. This is a daily growth experience, and I encourage you to do the same.

Take a moment to do a quick self-assessment.

1. What is your relationship with the person or persons who pluck your nerves the most?

2. How often does this person(s) annoy you?

3. What action or behavior does this person(s) demonstrate that tests your nerves?

4. How much of what plucks your nerve the most with this person(s) is controllable by the individual(s)?

5. What role do you play in the situation?

6. What measures have you taken to discuss your annoyance with the person(s) if any?

7. Think of any actions that person(s) has taken to not pluck your nerves so much.

Reflect on your responses to these questions. Although your loved one plucks your nerves at times, what are some things you can do to rise above the annoyance and not feel so exasperated with every encounter? There are tips and tools you can leverage to manage the frustration you feel when your loved one plucks your nerves. A few of the things I have learned over the years include effective communication, validation or encouragement, active listening, conflict resolution, self-care, meditation, deep breathing, exercise, and prayer. There are more practices, resources, and tools to pull from. You may consider seeking counseling or a life coach. Even though your loved ones might benefit from your new approach for managing annoying behavior, you likely will benefit the most on so many levels in your health and wellbeing.

Sis, before I end this letter, I encourage you to seek refuge in the Lord. I leave you with a few scriptures that will guide you with dealing with frustration and those who pluck your nerves.

Proverbs 10:12	1 Corinthians 13:4-7
Proverbs 15:1-7	Ephesians 4:2
Matthew 7:3-4	Ephesians 4:15
Luke 6:27-36	Colossians 4:6
John 15:12	2 Timothy 2:23-26
John 16:33	1 Peter 3:9
Romans 12:9-21	1 Peter 4:8

May the Word of God uplift and guide you on your journey to living your best life.

Check Their Motives and Yours

Letter 32

Dear Sis:

Have you encountered a situation where someone did the right thing but had an ulterior motive? What about you? Have you done the right thing for an ulterior motive? Having an ulterior motive is not a bad thing when you are honest, truthful, and have positive intent and wellbeing. The problem lies with doing the right thing and having a negative, hidden agenda or ill intent. To this I say, check your motives. Actions we take to do the right thing should be pure, in the best interest of ourselves and others, and pleasing to the Lord.

There are countless references in the Holy Bible that speak to the will of God and appropriate actions we should take as disciples of Christ. One example is Colossians 3:17, where the pericope of scripture says, "Whatever you do in word or deed, do all in the name of the Lord Jesus, giving thanks through him to God the Father." God takes time to call us out about wrong motives. According to James 4:3 (NASB), "You ask and do not receive, because you ask with wrong motives, so that you may spend it on your pleasures." In essence, he tells us that wrong motives block our blessings because of self-gratification or fleshly desires. Motives should be guilt-free and in love, according to the Lord's definition and not our version of love.

Sis, doing the right thing with wrong motives can lead you and others in the wrong direction. Again, I say, check their motives and yours. Motives can be directed by the individual's moral compass and core values. Perchance the Holy Bible is not your go-to reference. Think about times where someone did something for you that was good, and later you found out their malicious or selfish intent. How did that make you feel?

Let us consider the idea of someone promoting another in the workplace who meets all criteria and more. The leader promoted this person not because he or she was a great fit or deserved it. This person was promoted because the leader has intentions of using them to do their work so they can slack off and take all the credit. In fact, they plan to use that person as a fall guy. Check their motives. Perhaps someone invited an acquaintance to an event to be inclusive but thought it would be fun to tease or poke fun of that someone for laughs throughout the evening. Maybe you have done something nice for someone to make yourself look good, like participating in a charity event so you could get accolades for an organization you want to join. You know full well that this is not something you routinely do or care to do, but it is necessary for you to even be considered. Check your motives.

Keep Proverbs 16:2 (AMP) at the forefront of your mind when you desire to do something right but for egotistical reasons. This scripture says, "All the ways of a man are clean and innocent in his own eyes [and he may see nothing wrong with his actions], But the Lord weighs and examines the motives and intents [of the heart and knows the truth]." Sometimes you mean well but unconsciously have an ulterior motive that is wrong. You must do a gut check or self-check before you act. Make sure you are on the right side of doing things for the right reason. Ask yourself:

- Will God be glorified in doing this action?

- Will my actions cause hurt, harm, or danger?

- Will my actions make me feel good or guilty?

- What does God's Word say about motives?

- What direction does my moral compass lead me?

Sis, also leverage your circle of wisdom who you know has your best interest at heart. Take time for self-reflection and self-love. Most importantly, humbly go before the Lord in prayer about every move you want to make.

Pray this special prayer:
Lord, I come to you humbly thanking you for your grace, mercy, love, and wisdom. If I have committed any sins of commission or omission, I ask for your forgiveness. Create in me a clean heart and clear my mind from voices of confusion. Guide my footsteps in all that I do. Let your Word resonate loudly within me as I continue to seek you and be pleasing in your eyes. Allow savory words to flow from my mouth and your light to illuminate from within so that I may draw others to you. Allow your Holy Spirit to keep my moral compass on the straight and narrow path, and when I do wrong remind me of my purpose. Surround me with godly advisers who have my best interest at heart. Strengthen me where I may be able to endure stumbling blocks that may come my way. Help me to be obedient to your Word. Lord, these and all things I ask in your righteous and holy name. Amen

Anxiety Sucks, But You Are a Conqueror

Dear Sis:

Anxiety sucks, and you cannot begin to understand it until you go through or support someone who faces attacks. Some infrequent, but mild anxiety is normal given the circumstances. However, there are people diagnosed and undiagnosed with an anxiety disorder who experience various symptoms that many people do not understand. Anxiety is a feeling of nervousness, worry, or uneasiness usually about an impending event or something with an uncertain outcome.

According to the Anxiety & Depression Association of America (ADAA), people with General Anxiety Disorder (GAD) have "persistent and excessive worry about a number of different things, such as anticipation of disaster and feeling excessively concerned about money, health, family, work, or other issues" (para 1). It is oftentimes a challenge for people with GAD to control their worry, and their depth of worries is much more than necessary and maybe for no reason (ADAA). Anxiety levels can range from mild to moderate to more serious disorders.

Sis, I am not sure how much you know or understand about GAD, but more people are affected than you may realize. Statistically speaking, approximately seven million adults or approximately 3 percent of the U.S. population are affected by GAD (ADAA). In addition, women are most affected. I am a living witness to that. My anxiety was brought on by years of carrying stress on my shoulders until one day out of nowhere I was literally brought to my knees. I experienced a severe anxiety attack and panic attack all at once. I could not see or think straight. I was breathing rapidly on the verge of hyperventilation. On top of all that, the room was spinning, my heart was racing, and my body was trembling and sweating. It was difficult to focus. I could not let anyone see me like that. As a nurse, I knew what was happening and had to make my way home with the hope of feeling safe and getting myself together. By the grace of God, I made it home safely. That day is when my GAD began. It has been several years, and I have come a long way and can better manage my anxiety due to medication management, exercise, meditation and prayer, self-care, physical activity, getting proper sleep and relaxation, and other lifestyle changes. It also helps to have a strong support system and be aware of your triggers.

Even though I have GAD, I realize that I am not weak, but I am a survivor and fighter. I am stronger, wiser, and more than a conqueror. I hold on to this because of God's written Word in Romans 8:37 (NIV). His Word also tells me, "Do not fear, for I am with you; do not anxiously look about you. For I am your God. I will strengthen you. Surely, I will help you, surely I will uphold you with My righteous right hand" (Isaiah 41:10 NASB). This may be my cross to bear, but I am so thankful for how the Lord has orchestrated my care plan and the tools to help me each day.

Maybe you or someone you know has been diagnosed with a form of anxiety disorder. It is nothing to be ashamed of or shun someone because of mental health taboos. We are flawed beings, but we do not have to become a recluse, feel subpar, or label individuals as a defect. We simply realize our humanity and the importance of taking better care of ourselves as anyone else who has medical issues or physical disorders. Your condition does not define who you are. The Lord has already declared that we are victorious through Christ Jesus and that we can do all things through him who strengthens us. So, yes Sis, anxiety sucks, but each of us is a conqueror!

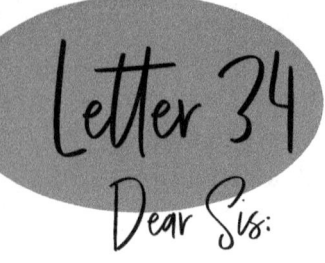

The Power of Words

Dear Sis:

Words matter because they are powerful and can change all moods, change the atmosphere, uplift, destroy, open and close doors, and more. If you do not believe me, consider the words in your favorite book. They can take your mind to all sorts of places, sway your emotional response, and inspire you. Words of a politician can draw a crowd to listen and even influence your decision. Words can provide knowledge and build skills. Words can help form and destroy relationships. There are more examples to pull from that speak to the power of words.

You can find a plethora of texts on the power of words. If you turn to God's Word, you will find various pericope of scriptures on this subject matter. Some of them are:

- Proverbs 15:4 (MSG): "Kind words heal and help; cutting words wound and maim."

- Proverbs 18:21 (MSG): "Words kill, words give life; they're either poison or fruit—you choose."

- Psalm 19:14 (ESV): "Let the words of my mouth and the meditation of my heart be acceptable in your sight, O Lord, my rock and my redeemer."

- Matthew 12:37 (ESV): "For by your words you will be justified, and by your words you will be condemned."

- Ephesians 4:29 (MSG): "Watch the way you talk. Let nothing foul or dirty come out of your mouth. Say only what helps, each word a gift."

- James 3:5 (ESV): "So also the tongue is a small member, yet it boasts of great things. How great a forest is set ablaze by such a small fire!

Even outside of the Bible, there are numerous books published on the power of words. Many of them speak to how words can affect you or something. Some speak to the sensibility of words. Some speak to the outcomes from words people use. Other literature or media used for advertisement not only use imagery, but they use keywords and phrases to lure the audience. Words can be subliminal in things we see and read.

Since words are a form of expression, we must use them wisely. Two primary functions that come to mind with words are 1) to build and 2) to destroy. Words used to build also construct, engage, and develop in extent. However, words used to destroy also put an end to existence by damaging or attacking and ruining someone or something completely. Sis, as individuals we must choose whether we want to be an architect or demolition woman.

- An architect builds by using verbal praise, positive/warm tone, sincere expression, and truth.
- A demolition woman destroys by using words of ridicule and negative/harsh tone, as well as to be two-faced and tell lies.

The choice is up to you, so choose wisely!

EXERCISES

Self-Love Inventory

Dear Sis: You are a beautiful, intelligent, dynamic Queen. To be the best version of yourself, it is important to do a self-love inventory. Take time to assess and reflect using the inventory check questions.

1. What comes to mind when you hear the word self-love?

   _____

   _____

   _____

   _____

   _____

   _____

2. Describe five things you love about yourself. Then describe at least three things that you love about your circle of friends (Queens) that compliments your friendship.

   _____

   _____

   _____

   _____

3. On a scale of 1-5, how important is taking time for yourself with the many hats you wear?

(1 = Not Important, 2 = Slightly Important, 3 = Important, 4 = Fairly Important, 5 = Very Important)

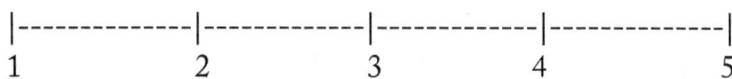

4. Considering your rank of importance, is there a need to make some adjustments to have time for yourself? If yes, describe some things you want to change and how you plan to commit to more self-love. If no, take some time to think of one thing you would like to do (more of) to treat yourself.

_____

_____

_____

_____

_____

5. Write at least three affirmations in which you can commit to being the best version of yourself.

_____

_____

_____

_____

_____

6. List at least three things you can do to support other Queens.

_____

_____

_____

_____

_____

7. If I had to choose one Queen who inspires me, I would choose _____

because she _____

_____

_____

_____

8. The one Dear Sis Letter that resonated the most with me is _____

because _____

_____

_____

_____

9. Identify your top three goals and where you are now in the process to achieve them. Describe any key actions you need to take to meet them.

_____

_____

_____

_____

_____

10. In doing this self-love inventory, I learned

_____

_____

_____

_____

_____

Sis, now that you have had the opportunity to complete your self-love inventory, take time to follow through on any takeaways you have outlined. Do not let this exercise be the last inventory. As you continue to grow and learn in life, always take time to appreciate the Queen you are. Also take time to uplift and celebrate other Queens.

Many people say I am my sister's keeper. If that is a declaration you make, mean it and apply it.

Please join me in prayer.

Heavenly Father, I pray now that every discovery this beautiful Sister has made while exploring each letter blesses her more than she imagined. Lord, let these God-spoken letters ignite a fire in her. Let every nugget this beautiful Sis has gained fuel her mind, heart, and soul, and inspire her to encourage other Queens. I ask, Lord, to strengthen and cover this woman of distinction from the top of her head to the sole of her feet.

I pray that she will draw closer to you, Lord, and walk in authority according to your will and your way. Let the words of her mouth and the meditation of her heart be pleasing in your sight. Touch her and her family and supply all their needs. Place your hedge of protection all around them. Lord, let her feel love and peace that only you can give. Continue to extend your grace and mercy over her life and those she touches. Let your light illuminate brightly through her so that others will see you — her Power Source.

If it is in your will, give her some of the desires of her heart that do not detract from who you have called her to be. As she continues to seek you, Lord, let everything she touches be fruitful and a reflection of you. I pray that your beautiful Queen remembers to give you all the honor, glory, and praise in all that she does. This is my sincere and humble prayer in your righteous and holy name. In the name of Jesus, I pray. Amen

Celebrate a Queen Calendar

Select a month to celebrate a queen each day. Some suggestions you may consider include: a compliment, shout out, pay for lunch or coffee/tea, surprise someone with a phone call or visit, write a letter or send a card, highlight someone on social media, buy a simple but thoughtful gift, and offer help. There are 100 ways or more to show kindness or celebrate another queen. Add action items to your calendar and make it happen. By the end of the month assess the outcomes from your experience.

SUN	MON	TUES	WED	THUR	FRI	SAT

You made it a whole month celebrating others queen or another sister. Describe your experience and where do you go from here.

_____

_____

_____

_____

_____

Crossword Puzzle: Building Faith Muscles

```
T Z W I I F K B L C K Q H G R Y F M P V B A B X M L W S M V
E E K R W J E R O J V N W K C O E M O A V I B S G Q T L X T
L S S H G E B N U D K W G N F W L B U P T G B N P U H B Y N
E S N T X W F K N Y W H N I Z L L O W M U I I L D G Z G L Z
B S F S I E X E Y E N N S V E D O H Z G E D E Y E K I N O N
U N F K S M Y Z M W C G O E P N W G Q J L W O N H L E I H C
U A F S F P O N E X X W V C Y Y S B O I O P G S C U H V B V
F Z I K Q L T N X Z C Y H G M N H M U D B Z P Z Q E E E O H
F O G S T V K U I C U M X F V T I B N B S E D B T I E I S L
N T S X U S R S G E I V E A C X P D E S U C O F S X V L K N
U I X I R Z I N D L S L Y S O J B E Z U V V I G E I D E I U
H P Z U V V G R Q R I Z B T U Y E K H K K G H L W N K B N G
O A Q F B X G U H I G X S I E K L J T T H R F K I Q J T H N
M Q G U R J L G J C H S U N Z W Y T Q W W E J F A K I Z E H
W O R D O Q X D X D E E I G S V A K W I K Y G U S R H Z A F
R R K E N L Z V Q N A R X J J N A K T M O A X A I C U I N K
P E Z K H H V L L M E D I T A T E N W X M R E P T H F O J N
R Z D T I K N U F C F G T S A A E A E V L P S Q Y Y B H X O
T O J N Q N F T L O K C O W B S L I J E C I F I R C A S A Y
B U D O E H I S O B W K A M S D D H Q Y A A R M S J X H W G
G G G Q T R A R M O R Y G N M N C J U E W B Z F G V H U G Y
Y A D I U V R D T J F B V R Y G T X P M N J H K X Y J V Z V
L P A V G W P U H S E Z M I Z T Z P A L T C N F W T T B W F
W F I H M Z P B S T M F L V R O B V P E J Q H A C P W Y S B
W I R G Q E U Z H K G A J Q Q Z C V G W M X R A D T U A M C
F O R G I V E N E S S I Z Z D T J A W F C U T G G N F E R Z
Y W E A N L A C M X R T I V I P J I W Q C R P L A H A A H S
C V W T S U R T H S Z H T Z Z P U G D Q O P L T I D O N R F
B Y A U B B L M L Z Y H W A X N O G K O X D N N M J D Q I K
O E O N A L Z V Q E F B N C W U F T G Z E O V N Y E M K B A
```

ARMOR
BELIEVING
BIBLE
BUILDING
CHRIST
CONFESSION
FAITH
FAITHFULNESS
FASTING
FELLOWSHIP
FLEX
FOCUSED
FORGIVENESS
GOD
HOLY
LOVE
MEDITATE
PATIENCE
PRAYER
SACRIFICE
SPIRIT
STUDY
SURRENDER
TESTIMONIES
TRUST
WITNESS
WORD

Solution

```
T + + + + + + + + C + + + + + F + P + B + + + + + S + +
+ E + + + + + + O + + + + + + E + + A + I + + G + T + + +
+ + S + + + + N + + + + + + + L + + + T + B N + U + + Y +
+ + + T + + F + + + + + + + + L + + + + I I L D + + G L +
+ + + + I E + + + + + + + + + O + + + + D E Y E + + N O +
+ + + + S M + + + + + + + + + W G + + L + + N + + E I H +
+ + + S + + O + + + + + + + + S + O I + + + + C + + V + +
+ + I + + + + N + + + + + + + H + U D + + + + + E + E O +
+ O + + T + + + I + + + + F + + I B + + + + + + + + I + L
N + + + + S + + + E + + + A + + P D E S U C O F + X + L +
+ + + + + + + I + + + S + + S + + + + + + + + + + E + + E +
+ + + + + + + + R + + + + + T + + + + + + + + + L + + B + +
+ + + + + + + + + H + + + S I + + + + + + + + R F + + + T + +
+ + + + + + + + + C + S + N + + + + + + W E + + + + I + + +
W O R D + + + + + + + E + + G + + + + + I + Y + + + R + + +
R + + + + + + + + + N + + + + + + + T + + A + + I + + + + +
+ E + + + + + + L M E D I T A T E N + + + R + P + + + + + +
+ + D + + + + U + + + + + + + + E + + + + P S + + + + + + +
+ + + N + + F + + + + + + + + S + + + E C I F I R C A S + +
+ + + + E H + + + + + + + + + S + + + + + + + + + + + + + +
+ + + + T R A R M O R + + + + + + + + + + + + + + + + + + +
+ + + I + + R + + + + + + + + + + + + + + + + + + + + + + +
+ + A + + + + U + + + + + + + + + + + + + + + + + + + + + +
+ F + + + + + S + + F + + + + + + + + + + + + + + + + + + +
+ + + + + + + + + + A + + + + + + + + + + + + + + + + + + +
F O R G I V E N E S S I + + + + + + + + + + + + + + + + + +
+ + + + + + + + + + + T + + + + + + + + + + + + + + + + + +
+ + + T S U R T + + + H + + + + + + + + + + + + + + + + + +
+ + + + + + + + + + + + + + + + + + + + + + + + + + + + + +
+ + + + + + + + + + + + + + + + + + + + + + + + + + + + + +
```

(Over, Down, Direction)		
ARMOR (7,21,E)	FLEX (23,13,NE)	SPIRIT (23,18,NE)
BELIEVING (28,12,N)	FOCUSED (24,10,W)	STUDY (28,1,SW)
BIBLE (21,1,SE)	FORGIVENESS (1,26,E)	SURRENDER (9,24,NW)
BUILDING (18,9,NE)	GOD (18,6,SE)	TESTIMONIES (1,1,SE)
CHRIST (10,14,NW)	HOLY (29,6,N)	TRUST (8,28,W)
CONFESSION (10,1,SW)	LOVE (30,9,NW)	WITNESS (21,14,SW)
FAITH (12,24,S)	MEDITATE (10,17,E)	WORD (1,15,E)
FAITHFULNESS (2,24,NE)	PATIENCE (19,1,SE)	
FASTING (14,9,S)	PRAYER (22,18,N)	
FELLOWSHIP (17,1,S)	SACRIFICE (28,19,W)	

Maze Exercise: It is All About Direction

This puzzle exercise focuses on following the path laid before you. Remember that the Lord orders your steps and leads you to the path of righteousness. When you go in your own direction, it will take you down different paths just to end up where the Lord's straight and narrow path would have gotten you there much sooner.

Solution

Fallen Phrases Exercise: The Power of Words Puzzle

Every word uttered from our mouths should be savory. As Queens, let us be mindful to uplift one another and speak life.

Solution

Bible Translations

Scripture	Translation	Description
1 Corinthians 13:4-7		All Translations
1 Corinthians 2:9	GW	God's Word
1 John 4:18	NIV	New International Version
1 Peter 3:9		All Translations
1 Peter 4: 10	NASB1995	New American Standard Bible 1995
1 Peter 4:8		All Translations
1 Peter 5:7	NIV	New International Version
1 Samuel 16	NIV	New International Version
1 Thessalonians 5:11	NIV	New International Version
1 Thessalonians 4:13-14	NIV	New International Version
2 Corinthians 12:9	NIV	New International Version
2 Corinthians 3:5	NLT	New Living Translation
2 Corinthians 5:7	NIV	New International Version
2 Corinthians 9:15	NASB1996	New American Standard Bible 1995
2 Corinthians 9:8	NLT	New Living Translation
2 Corinthians 9:8	MSG	The Message
2 Kings 20:5	NIV	New International Version
2 Timothy 2:23-26		All Translations
Acts 17:28	ASV	American Standard Version
Colossians 4:6	NIV	New International Version
Colossians 4:6		All Translations
Deuteronomy 31:18	NIV	New International Version
Deuteronomy 31:6	MSG	The Message
Ephesians 4:15		All Translations
Ephesians 4:2		All Translations
Ephesians 4:29	MSG	The Message
Ephesians 4:31-32	ESV	English Standard Version
Ephesians 6:10-18	NIV	New International Version

Bible Translations

Scripture	Translation	Description
Ephesians 6:14-17	NIV	New International Version
Galatians 5:22	NIV	New International Version
Galatians 5:23	NIV	New International Version
Genesis1: 26-27	NIV	New International Version
Hebrews 13:8	NIV	New International Version
Isaiah 25:1	ESV	English Standard Version
Isaiah 41:10	NASB1995	New American Standard Bible 1995
Isaiah 41:10	MSG	The Message
Isaiah 43:1	NIV	New International Version
Isaiah 54:17	MEV	Modern English Version
Isaiah 64:4	NIV	New International Version
James 1:19	ESV	English Standard Version
James 3:16	ESV	English Standard Version
James 3:5	ESV	English Standard Version
James 4:3	NASB	New American Standard Bible
Jeremiah 29:11	NIV	New International Version
Jeremiah 33:3	NIV	New International Version
Job 1: 6-22	NIV	New International Version
John 15:12		All Translations
John 16:33		All Translations
Luke 22:31	NIV	New International Version
Luke 6:27-28	ESV	English Standard Version
Luke 6:27-36		All Translations
Luke 6:31	NIV	New International Version
Matthew 12:33	NIV	New International Version
Matthew 12:37	ESV	English Standard Version
Matthew 5:4	NIV	New International Version
Matthew 7:3-4		All Translations
Philippians 2:3	CSB	Christian Standard Bible

Bible Translations

Scripture	Translation	Description
Philippians 2:3	ESV	English Standard Version
Philippians 4:13	NKJV	New King James Version
Proverbs 10:12		All Translations
Proverbs 15:1-7		All Translations
Proverbs 15:4	MSG	The Message
Proverbs 16:2	AMP	Amplified Bible
Proverbs 16:3	MSG	The Message
Proverbs 16:9	NIV	New International Version
Proverbs 17:17	NIV	New International Version
Proverbs 17:22	ESV	English Standard Version
Proverbs 18:21	MSG	The Message
Proverbs 3:6	NIV	New International Version
Proverbs 6:34	ESV	English Standard Version
Psalm 133:1	NIV	New International Version
Psalm 139:14	NIV	New International Version
Psalm 18:2	NIV	New International Version
Psalm 18:2	NIV	New International Version
Psalm 19:14	ESV	English Standard Version
Psalm 25:4	NIV	New International Version
Psalm 27:1-2	NIV	New International Version
Psalm 27:1-2	AMP	Amplified Bible
Psalm 27:5	NIV	New International Version
Psalm 32:8	NIV	New International Version
Psalm 34:10	NKJV	New King James Version
Psalm 34:18	AMP	Amplified Bible
Psalm 34:18	NIV	New International Version
Psalm 37:7	NIV	New International Version
Romans 10:9	NIV	New International Version
Romans 12:2	ESV	English Standard Version

Endnotes

1. Robin A. Cohen, Ph.D., Amy E. Cha, Ph.D., M.P.H., Michael E. Martinez, M.P.H., M.H.S.A., and Emily P. Terlizzi, M.P.H. (2019). Health Insurance Coverage: Early Release of Estimates From the National Health Interview Survey, 2019. *National Center for Health Statistics*, 1-18.

2. Betty-Ann Heggie. (2019). The Healing Power of Laughter. *Journal of hospital medicine*, *14*(5), 320.

3. Mayo Clinic Staff. (2019, April 5). Stress relief from laughter? it's no joke. *Health Lifestyle Stress Management*

4. Rachel Cosgrove, C.S.C.S. (2015). 10 Ways to Gain Muscle. Men's Fitness.

5. Neal-Barnett, A., Stadulis, R., Murray, M., Payne, M. R., Thomas, A., & Salley, B. B. (2011). Sister Circles as a Culturally Relevant Intervention for Anxious African American Women. *Clinical psychology: a publication of the Division of Clinical Psychology of the American Psychological Association*, 18(3), 266–273.

Bibliography

Robin A. Cohen, Ph.D., Amy E. Cha, Ph.D., M.P.H., Michael E. Martinez, M.P.H., M.H.S.A., and Emily P. Terlizzi, M.P.H. "Health Insurance Coverage: Early Release of Estimates From the National Health Interview Survey, 2019." *National Center for Health Statistics* (2019): 1-18. https://www.cdc.gov/nchs/data/nhis/earlyrelease/insur202009-508.pdf.

Betty-Ann Heggie. "The Healing Power of Laughter." *Journal of hospital medicine*, *14*(5) (2019): 320. https://doi.org/10.12788/jhm.3205.

Mayo Clinic Staff. "Stress relief from laughter? it's no joke." *Health Lifestyle Stress Management* (April 5, 2019). depth/stress-relief/art-20044456.

Rachel Cosgrove, C.S.C.S. "10 Ways to Gain Muscle." *Men's Fitness* (2015). http://www.mensfitness.com/training/build-muscle/10-ways-to-gain-muscle0/

Neal-Barnett, A., Stadulis, R., Murray, M., Payne, M. R., Thomas, A., & Salley, B. B. "Sister Circles as a Culturally Relevant Intervention for Anxious African American Women." *Clinical psychology: a publication of the Division of Clinical Psychology of the American Psychological Association*, 18(3) (2011):, 266–273. https://doi.org/10.1111/j.1468-2850.2011.01258.x

About the Author

Author, entrepreneur, educator, and seasoned healthcare professional, Dr. Latosha P. Burch is the author of Dear Sis: Letters to a Queen. She is a wife, mother, sister, and friend. Dr. Burch is a native of Clio, South Carolina, but Virginia has been her home for more than 16 years. She and her husband have a blended family of five children, who are all grown, and three beautiful grandchildren. Dr. Burch enjoys spending time with her family, playing fun but challenging games, praise dancing, shopping, and vacationing.

Dr. Burch also has approximately 25 years in the health care industry and 15 years as an Adjunct Professor. She has several significant credentials including Doctor of Health Administration (DHA) from Capella University, Master of Education in Instruction Technology (MSE IT) from Kaplan University; Master of Health Administration (MHA), and a Bachelor of Science in Health Administration (BSHA) from the University of Phoenix; and Diploma of Health Science in Practice Nursing from Northeastern Technical College. She holds licensure as a Licensed Practical Nurse (LPN) and various certifications as a Professional Life Coach (PLC), Basic Life Support & First Aid Instructor (BLS & FA), ISTQB Certified Tester Foundation Level (CTFL), SAFe Scaled Agilist (SA), Certified Scrum Master (SSM), and a volunteer Community Health Worker (CHW) and Virginia Medical Reserve Corp (MRC).

Dr. Burch is active in her community as a Deaconess at her church St. Mark Missionary Baptist Church, and is a finer woman of Zeta Phi Beta Sorority, Inc. She has diligently served in various leadership and community service roles.

She is a lover of the Lord and thankful for the opportunity to witness and serve as a disciple of Christ. Dr. Burch has served with the Medical Reserve Corp for more than 15 years and volunteered as a Community Health Worker for the local health department for several years. Serving is a blessing and a ministry to Dr. Burch.